Fod

frankfurt

MW00452392

Portions of this book appear in *Fodor's Germany*

fodor's travel publications
new york • toronto • london • sydney • auckland
www.fodors.com

contents

maps

ON THE ROAD WITH FODOR'S

EVERY VACATION IS IMPORTANT. So here at Fodor's we've pulled out all stops in preparing *Fodor's Pocket Frankfurt*. To help you zero in on what to see in Frankfurt, we've created great multiday itineraries and neighborhood walks. Having seen all corners of Frankfurt, our writer is a real expert.

Ted Shoemaker settled in Germany more than 40 years ago when, as a U.S. Army officer, he married a German. He has been editor of three English-language magazines in Germany and a correspondent for many American publications. He lives in Frankfurt.

Don't Forget to Write

Keeping a travel guide fresh and up-to-date is a big job. So we love your feedback—positive and negative—and follow up on all suggestions. Contact the *Pocket Frankfurt* editor at editors@fodors.com or c/o Fodor's, 280 Park Avenue, New York, New York 10017. And have a wonderful trip!

Karen Cure

Karen Cure

Editorial Director

germany

DENMARK

North Sea

Baltic Sea

Flensburg
Husum
Fehmarn
Kiel
Rügen
Rostock
Barth
Stralsund
Neustadt
Greifswald
Cuxhaven
Anklam
Caroliensiel
Güstrow
Teterow
Neubrandenburg
Norden
Wismar
Waren
Wilhelmshaven
Schwerin
Emden
Bremerhaven
Hamburg
Neustadt-Glewe
Neustrelitz
HOLLAND
Oldenburg
Bremen
Ludwigslust
Meppen
FORMER BORDER
BETWEEN EAST AND
WEST GERMANY
Pritzwalk
Perleberg
Neuruppin
Salzwedel
Wittenberge
Oranienburg
Rheine
Osnabrück
Hannover
Wolfsburg
Stendal
Brandenburg
Berlin
Minden
Braunschweig
Magdeburg
Potsdam
Frankfurt am
der Oder
Münster
Bielefeld
Hildesheim
Halberstadt
Lübben
Duisberg
Essen
Dortmund
Göttingen
Nordhausen
Bernburg
Dessau
Wittenberg
Bitterfeld
Cottbus
Hagen
Kassel
Halle
Leipzig
Meissen
Görlitz
Düsseldorf
Mühlhausen
Aachen
Köln
Siegen
Bad Hersfeld
Erfurt
Weimar
Gera
Dresden
Bonn
Marburg
Eisenach
Chemnitz
Giessen
Alsfeld
Suhl
Saalfeld
Zwickau
Fulda
Meiningen
Plauen
Koblenz
Wilhelmsbad
Steinau an
der Strasse
Hof
Wiesbaden
Hanau
Coburg
Münchberg
Trier
Mainz
Frankfurt-am-Main
Bingen
Darmstadt
Würzburg
Bamberg
Bayreuth
CZECH REPUBLIC
Bad
Kreuznach
Mannheim
Fürth
Saarbrücken
Ludwigshafen
Heidelberg
Nürnberg
Speyer
Rothenburg-
o-d-Tauber
Regensburg
Deggendorf
Karlsruhe
Heilbronn
Straubing
FRANCE
Baden-Baden
Stuttgart
Offenburg
Tübingen
Ulm
Danube
Augsburg
Passau
Neu-Ulm
Munich
Freiburg
Biberach
Memmingen
Isar
Inn
Tuttlingen
Bodensee
Ravensburg
Bad Reichenhall
Rheinfelden
Konstanz
Wangen
Friedrichshafen
Garmisch-
Partenkirchen
Berchtesgaden

SWITZERLAND

AUSTRIA

LICHTENSTEIN

ITALY

Elbe · *Oder* · *Neisse* · *Ems* · *Rhine* · *Mosel* · *Main* · *Rhein* · *Donau*

POLAND

0   100 miles
0   150 km

N

Gräfstr.

Eppsteinerstr.

Reuterweg

Leerbachstr.

Trutz

Gärtnerw

U WESTEND Staufenstr.

Bockenheimer Landstr.

Unterlindau

Oberlindau

Rothschild Park

Bockenheimer

An

Schumannstr.

Beethovenstr.

Lindenstr.

WESTEND

ALTE OPER

Kettenhofweg

Seckenbergeranlage

Kettenhofweg

U

Opernplatz

Fressg

Westendstr.

Mendelssohnstr.

Guiolettestr.

Goethest.

Hamburger Allee

U MESSE

Westend pl.

Taunusanlage

Junghofstr.

Friedrich Ebert-Anlage

Rheinstr.

Niederau

S TAUNUS-ANLAGE

Neue Mainzer Str.

Gr. Gallusstr.

Messegelände

Savignystr.

Westendstr.

Zimmerweg

Taunusanl.

Taunus-tor

Gallusanl.

Mainzer Landstr.

Düssel-dorfestr.

Karlstr.

Taunusstr.

Weserstr.

W.-BRANDT-PL.

U

Frieden-str.

Weiss frauen

Haupt-bahnhof

Am Hauptbahnhof

Kaiserstr.

Münchenerstr.

i

S U HAUPTBNHF.

Gutleutstr.

Mannheimerstr.

Baseler str.

Wilhelm Leuschner Str.

Untermainkai

Holbein-steg

Main

Schaumainkai

Gutleutstr.

Hafenstr.

Friedensbr.

Stresemannallee

Kennedyallee

Sch

Westhafen

Thorwaldsenstr.

Bu

KEY

i Tourist Information

s S-Bahn

u U-Bahn

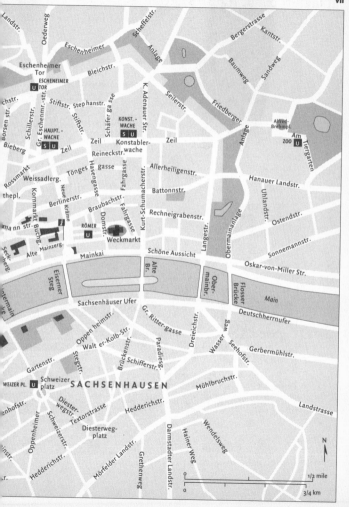

frankfurt public transit system

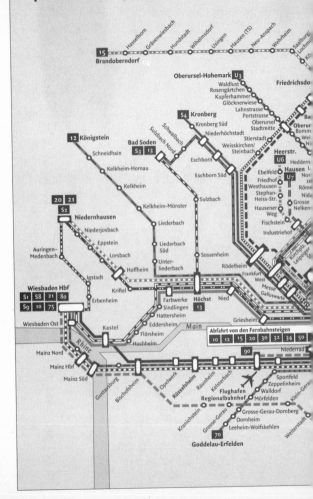

frankfurt

introducing frankfurt

WITH A LONG HISTORY as a banking and trade center, Frankfurt redesigned itself as a modern city after the ravages of World War II, putting more energy into raising skyscrapers than reconstructing its medieval Old Town. Although modest in size (fifth among German cities, with a population of 652,000), the city cheekily nicknamed itself Mainhattan, using the name of the Main River that flows through it to suggest the famous metropolis across the Atlantic. Five of Germany's largest banks make their headquarters here, as well as the German Central Bank (Bundesbank). A total of 370 credit institutions (230 of them foreign banks) and the European Central Bank (ECB), which manages the euro, have offices in the city as well. You can see how the city acquired its other nickname: "Bankfurt am Main."

But even a city so closely tied to the day-to-day turns of the financial markets does have a pre-banking history. According to legend, a deer revealed the ford across the Main River to the Frankish emperor Charlemagne. A stone ridge, now blasted away, made the shallow river a great conduit for trade and by the early 13th century Frankfurt ("ford of the Franks") had emerged as a major trading center. Frankfurt's first international Autumn Fair was held in 1240; in 1330 it added a Spring Fair. Today, these and other trade shows exhibit the latest in books, cars, consumer goods, and technology. The city's stock exchange, one of the half-dozen most important in the world, was established in 1585, and the Rothschild family opened its first bank here in 1798.

So why come to Frankfurt if not on business? Partly for its history, which spans more than 1,200 years. It was one of the joint capitals of Charlemagne's empire; the city where Holy Roman emperors were elected and crowned; the site of Gutenberg's print shop; the birthplace of Goethe (1749–1832), Germany's greatest poet; and the city where the first German parliament met. The Römerberg is the city's medieval heart, where evidence of a long history is most palpable. Take a look at the Römer, or city hall, and its Kaisersaal before admiring the magnificent Gothic carvings of the Kaiserdom (cathedral). In the Historisches Museum you can study a perfect scale model of old Frankfurt.

Because of all its commercialism, Frankfurt has a reputation for being crass, cold, and boring. But people who know the city find this characterization unfair. The district of Sachsenhausen is as *Gemütlich* (fun, friendly, and cozy) as you will find anywhere. The city has world-class ballet, opera, theater, and art exhibitions; an important piece of Germany's publishing industry; a large university (35,000 students) famous for such modern thinkers as Adorno and Habermas; and two of Germany's three most important daily newspapers, the *Frankfurter Allgemeine* and the *Frankfurter Rundschau*.

Cross over the Eiserner Steg bridge to reach Sachsenhausen's museums, lined up like ducks in a row on the Main's south bank. The Städelsches Kunstinstitut und Städtische Galerie holds a famous collection of Old Masters and Impressionists, and the Städtische Galerie Liebieghaus has sculpture from the third millennium BC up to the modern age. The elbow-worn tables of neighborhood apple-cider taverns will be waiting for you once you've had your fill of culture.

In Frankfurt you'll find a sophisticated and cosmopolitan city. There may not be that much here to remind you of the Old World, but there's a great deal that explains Germany's postwar success story.

In This Chapter

here and there

MUSEUMS THAT ARE as interesting for their architecture as for their contents are Frankfurt's main tourist draw. Historic Sachsenhausen, which is largely residential, is home to seven of these museums. They line the south bank of the Main, on Schaumainkai, known locally as the Museumsufer (Museum Bank).

The area around the Hauptbahnhof (main train station) and adjoining Westend district are mostly devoted to business, and banks tower overhead. You'll find the department stores of the Hauptwache and Zeil only a few blocks east of the station, but avoid the drug-ridden red-light district, also near the station. The city's past can be found in the Old Town's restored medieval quarter.

Numbers in the text correspond to numbers in the margin and on the Exploring Frankfurt map.

CITY CENTER AND WESTEND

Frankfurt was rebuilt after World War II with little attention paid to its past, but historical monuments can still be found among the city's modern architectural masterpieces. The city is very walkable; its growth hasn't encroached on its parks, gardens, pedestrian arcades, and outdoor cafés. The largest banks cluster in the *Bankenviertel*, centered on Neue Mainzer Strasse, between the city center and Westend.

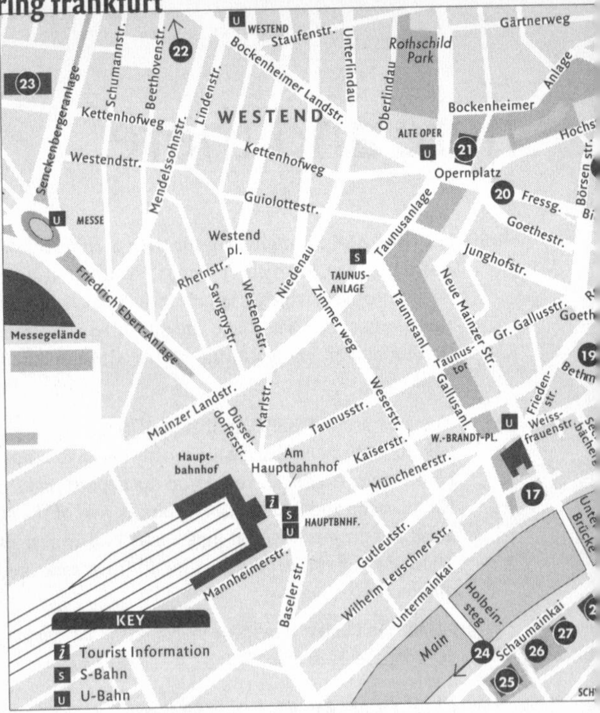

Map labels (as they appear on the map):

Gärtnerweg

WESTEND · Staufenstr. · Bockenheimer Landstr. · Unterlindau · Oberlindau · Rothschild Park · Bockenheimer · Anlage · Hochs

Schumannstr. · Beethovenstr. · Lindenstr. · Kettenhofweg · WESTEND · Kettenhofweg · ALTE OPER · Opernplatz · Börsen str.

Senckenberganlage · Mendelssohnstr. · Guiollettstr. · Fressg. · Goethestr. · Bi

Westendstr. · Westend pl. · Taunusanlage · Junghofstr.

MESSE · Rheinstr. · Niedenau · TAUNUS-ANLAGE · Neue Mainzer Str. · Gr. Gallusstr. · Goeth

Friedrich Ebert-Anlage · Savignystr. · Westendstr. · Zimmer weg · Taunusanl. · Taunus-tor · Gallusanl. · Friedens-str. · Bettm

Messegelände · Mainzer Landstr. · Düsseldorferstr. · Karlstr. · Taunusstr. · Weserstr. · W.-BRANDT-PL. · Weiss-frauenstr.

Haupt-bahnhof · Am Hauptbahnhof · Kaiserstr. · Münchenerstr.

HAUPTBHNHF. · Gutleutstr. · Wilhelm Leuschner Str.

Baseler str. · Untermainkai · Holbein-steg

KEY

Mannheimerstr. · Main · Schaumainkai · Unter · Brücke

i Tourist Information
S S-Bahn
U U-Bahn

City Center and Westend

Alte Oper, 21

Börse, 9

Eiserner Steg, 15

Fressgasse, 20

Goethehaus und Goethemuseum, 19

Hauptwache, 7

Historisches Museum, 4

Jüdisches Museum, 17

Kaiserdom, 13

Karmeliterkloster, 18

Katharinenkirche, 8

Leonhardskirche, 16

Liebfrauenkirche, 6

Museum für Moderne Kunst, 12

Naturkundemuseum Senckenberg, 23

Nikolaikirche, 3

Palmengarten und Botanischer Garten, 22

Paulskirche, 5

Römer, 2

Römerberg, 1

Schirn Kunsthalle, 14

Staufenmauer, 11

Zoologischer Garten, 10

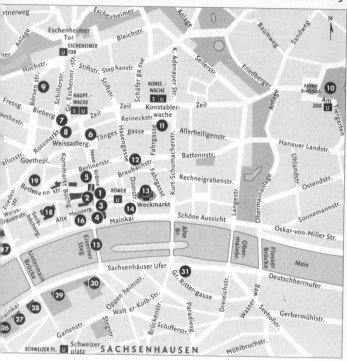

A Good Tour

Römerberg ①, the historic heart of Frankfurt, has been the center of civic life for centuries. Taking up most of the west side of the square is the city hall, called the **Römer** ②. It's a modest-looking building compared with many of Germany's other city halls. In the center of the square stands the fine 16th-century Fountain of Justice.

On the south side of the Römerberg is the red sandstone **Nikolaikirche** ③. Beside it stands the **Historisches Museum** ④, where you can see a perfect scale model of historic Frankfurt. On the east side of the square is the Ostzeile, a row of painstakingly restored half-timber houses dating from the 15th and 16th centuries.

From the Römerberg, walk up the pedestrian street called Neue Kräme. Looming up on the left is the circular bulk of the **Paulskirche** ⑤, a mostly 18th-century church more interesting for its political significance than as a place of worship. It was here that the short-lived German parliament met for the first time in May 1848. From the Paulskirche, keep heading along the Neue Kräme, which becomes Liebfrauenstrasse. In more peaceful surroundings stands the **Liebfrauenkirche** ⑥, a late-Gothic church dating from the end of the 14th century.

Liebfrauenstrasse ends at the **Hauptwache** ⑦, a square that is the hub of the city's transportation network, and is named after the 18th-century building that stands on it. The building's café can attend to your appetite if you need a break. A vast shopping mall also lies below the square. To the south of the Hauptwache is the **Katharinenkirche** ⑧, the most important Protestant church in the city. North of the Hauptwache, Schillerstrasse leads to the Börsenplatz and Frankfurt's leading stock exchange, the **Börse** ⑨.

The Hauptwache is also at the east end of the **Zeil,** Frankfurt's largest pedestrian zone and main shopping street. Its department stores sell every conceivable type of consumer goods and can get very crowded. A 15- to 20-minute walk all the way down the Zeil brings you to Alfred-Brehm-Platz and the entrance to the **Zoologischer Garten** ⑩. This is one of Frankfurt's chief attractions, ranking among the best zoos in Europe. If you don't want to walk the Zeil's full length, turn right at the square Konstabler Wache onto Fahrgasse. Follow the signs reading AN DER STAUFENMAUER to the **Staufenmauer** ⑪, one of the few surviving stretches of the old city wall.

Continue down Fahrgasse and turn right onto Battonstrasse. At the intersection of Battonstrasse and Domstrasse you'll see the striking wedge-shape outline of the **Museum für Moderne Kunst** ⑫. Walk south down Domstrasse a few steps and another silhouette appears, that of the **Kaiserdom** ⑬, the grand Gothic cathedral. An archaeological site next to the cathedral contains remains of Roman baths; from there walk through the pedestrian zone alongside the modern **Schirn Kunsthalle** ⑭, a major venue for art exhibitions.

Continue back to the Römerberg and turn left to get to the Mainkai, the busy street running parallel to the tree-lined Main River. On your left you will see the Rententurm, one of the city's medieval gates, with its pinnacled towers at the base of the main spire extending out over the walls. In front of you to your right is the **Eiserner Steg** ⑮, an iron footbridge connecting central Frankfurt with the old district of Sachsenhausen. River trips, boat excursions, and the old steam train leave from here.

Past the Eiserner Steg is the **Leonhardskirche** ⑯, which has one of the few 15th-century stained-glass windows to have survived World War II. Continue downstream, and just past the Untermainbrücke is the **Jüdisches Museum** ⑰ in the former Rothschild Palais, which focuses on the history of Frankfurt's Jewish community.

Backtrack a short way, then turn left into the narrow Karmelitergasse, which will take you to the **Karmeliterkloster** ⑱.

The monastery and its buildings house an museum of early history and the largest religious fresco north of the Alps. Exit onto Münzgasse, turn left, and proceed to the intersection of Bethmannstrasse and Berlinerstrasse. Use the pedestrian walkway and cross over to the north side of Berlinerstrasse; then turn left again onto Grosser Hirschgraben. At No. 23 there will probably be a small crowd outside the **Goethehaus und Goethemuseum** ⑲, where writer Johann Wolfgang von Goethe was born in 1749.

Leaving the Goethehaus, go to Goetheplatz and continue past the Gutenberg Memorial into the pedestrian zone to Rathenau-Platz. At the end of the square turn left again, this time onto Grosse Bockenheimer Strasse, known locally as **Fressgasse** ⑳ because of its many delicatessens, bakeries, and cafés.

Fressgasse ends at Opernplatz and the **Alte Oper** ㉑, a prime venue for classical concerts as well as conferences and, every now and then, an opera. From the steps of the opera house or the street Taunusanlage opposite are impressive views of Frankfurt's modern architecture. Looking down Taunusanlage, you'll see the twin towers of the Deutsche Bank (the two towers are known as *Zoll und Haben*, or "debit and credit"). The very tall building to the left, topped by an antenna, is the 849-ft Commerzbank, the tallest building in Europe. Between them is the Maintower, headquarters of the Hessische Landesbank and site of Frankfurt's first skyscraper rooftop restaurant.

Take the U-Bahn two stops from Alte Oper to Bockenheimer Warte, walk down Bockenheimer Landstrasse, and turn left on Palmengartenstrasse to reach the delightful **Palmengarten und Botanischer Garten** ㉒. Also close to the Bockenheimer Warte stop is the **Naturkundemuseum Senckenberg** ㉓, with fun hands-on exhibits.

TIMING

Count on spending a full day on this tour. Block out 45 minutes for each museum you choose to visit. If you intend to visit the Zoologischer Garten, expect to spend 1½ hours there.

What to See

㉑ ALTE OPER (Old Opera House). Kaiser Wilhelm I traveled from Berlin for the gala opening of the opera house in 1880. Gutted in World War II, the house remained a hollow shell for 40 years while controversy raged over its reconstruction. The exterior and lobby are faithful to the original, though the remainder of the building is more like a modern multi-purpose hall. Even if you don't go to a performance, it's worth having a look at the ponderous and ornate lobby, an example of 19th-century neoclassicism at its most self-confident. *Opernpl., tel. 069/134–0400, www.alte-oper-frankfurt.de.*

OFF THE BEATEN PATH **Alter Jüdischer Friedhof** (Old Jewish Cemetery)—The old Jewish quarter is east of Börneplatz, a short walk south of the Konstablerwache U-Bahn station or east of the Römer one. Partly vandalized during the Nazi era, the cemetery was in use between the 13th and 19th centuries and is one of the few reminders of prewar Jewish life in Frankfurt. To visit the old cemetery, you must go to the newer Jewish cemetery at Eckenheimer Landstrasse 238 (about a mile and a half north), leave some form of personal identification (like a passport), and pick up the key. (Quite a few Americans have ancestors buried at the newer cemetery.) *Kurt-Schumacher-Str. and Battonstr., tel. 069/561–826. Free. Daily 8:30–4:30.*

⑨ BÖRSE (Stock Exchange). This is the center of Germany's stock and money markets. The Börse was founded by Frankfurt merchants in 1585 to establish some order in their often chaotic dealings, but the present building dates from the 1870s. These days computerized networks and international telephone systems have removed some of the drama from the dealers' floor, but it is still an exciting scene to watch from the visitors' gallery. *Börsepl., tel. 069/21010, www.deutsche-boerse.com. Free. Visitors' gallery weekdays 10:30–1:30.*

⑮ EISERNER STEG (Iron Bridge). A pedestrian walkway and the first suspension bridge in Europe, the bridge connects the city center with Sachsenhausen.

ESCHENHEIMER TURM (Eschenheim Tower). Built in the early 15th century, this tower, a block north of the Hauptwache, remains the finest example of the city's original 42 towers. *Eschenheimer Tor.*

⑳ FRESSGASSE ("Pig-Out Alley"). Grosse Bockenheimer Strasse is the proper name of this pedestrian street, one of the city's liveliest thoroughfares, but Frankfurters have given it this sobriquet because of its amazing collection of delicatessens, wine merchants, cafés, and restaurants. Food shops offer fresh or smoked fish, cheeses, and a wide range of local specialties, including frankfurters. In summer you can sit at tables on the sidewalk and dine alfresco.

★ **⑲ GOETHEHAUS UND GOETHEMUSEUM** (Goethe's House and Museum). The house where Germany's most famous poet was born in 1749 is furnished with many original family pieces and displays original manuscripts. Though Goethe is most associated with Weimar, where he lived most of his life, Frankfurters are proud to claim him as a native son. The house was destroyed by Allied bombing but has been rebuilt and restored in every detail so that it is just as the young Goethe would have known it. Goethe studied law and became a member of the bar in Frankfurt but preferred the life of a writer and published his first best-seller, the drama *Götz von Berlichingen*, at the age of 20. He sealed his fame a few years later with the tragic love story *Die Leiden des Jungen Werthers* (The Sorrows of Young Werther). Goethe also wrote the first version of his masterpiece, *Faust*, in Frankfurt. The adjoining museum contains works of art that inspired Goethe (he was an amateur painter) and works associated with his literary contemporaries, members of the *Sturm und Drang* (Storm and Stress) movement. This circle of writers and artists abandoned neoclassical ideals for the darker world of human subjectivity, and helped create the romantic cult of the youthful genius in rebellion against society. *Grosser Hirschgraben 23–25, tel. 069/138–800. DM 7/€3.50. Apr.–Sept., weekdays 9–6, weekends 10–4; Oct.–Mar., weekdays 9–4, weekends 10–4.*

⑦ HAUPTWACHE. This square is where Grosse Bockeheimer Strasse (Fressgasse) runs into the Zeil, a main shopping street; a vast underground shopping mall stretches beneath it. The attractive Baroque building with a steeply sloping roof is the actual Hauptwache (Main Guardhouse). Built in 1729, it had been tastelessly expanded over the years and was demolished to permit the excavation for the mall and subway station beneath it. It was subsequently rebuilt in its original form. It now houses a café.

④ HISTORISCHES MUSEUM (History Museum). This fascinating museum encompasses all aspects of the city's history over the past eight centuries. It contains a scale model of historic Frankfurt, complete with every street, house, and church. There are also an astonishing display of silver and a children's museum with changing interactive exhibits. In a past exhibit, kids could play clerks and customers in a *Kaufladen*, a dollhouse-like depiction of a 19th-century grocery store. *Saalg. 19, tel. 069/2123–5599. DM 8/€4; free Wed. Tues. and Thurs.–Sun. 10–5, Wed. 10–8.*

⑰ JÜDISCHES MUSEUM (Jewish Museum). The story of Frankfurt's Jewish quarter is told in the former Rothschild Palais. Prior to the Holocaust, the city's Jewish community was the second largest in Germany. The museum contains extensive archives of Jewish history and culture, including a library of 5,000 books, a large photographic collection, and a documentation center. A branch of the museum, **Museum Judengasse** (Kurt-Schumacher-Str. 10, tel. 069/297–7419; DM 3/1.50; Tues. and Thurs.–Sun. 10–5, Wed. 10–8), is built around the foundations of mostly 18th-century buildings in what was once the ghetto. The branch is also near the Old Jewish Cemetery (☞ Alter Jüdischer Friedhof). *Untermainkai 14–15, tel. 069/2123–5000, www.juedischesmuseum.de. DM 5/€2.50. Tues. and Thurs.–Sun. 10–5, Wed. 10–8.*

⓫ KAISERDOM. Because Holy Roman Emperors were elected and crowned here from the 16th to the 18th centuries, the church is known as the Kaiserdom (Imperial Cathedral), even though it isn't the seat of a bishop. Officially the Church of St. Bartholomew, it was built largely between the 13th and 15th centuries and survived World War II with most of its treasures intact. It replaced a church established by Charlemagne's son, Ludwig the Pious, on the present site of the Römerberg. The many magnificent, original Gothic carvings include a life-size Crucifixion group and the fine 15th-century *Maria-Schlaf* (Altar of Mary Sleeping). The most impressive exterior feature is the tall, red-sandstone tower (almost 300 ft high), which was added between 1415 and 1514. It was the tallest structure in Frankfurt before the skyscrapers, and the view from the top is still of an exciting panorama. In 1953 excavation in front of the main entrance revealed the remains of a Roman settlement and the foundations of a Carolingian imperial palace. The **Dommuseum** (Cathedral Museum) occupies the former Gothic cloister. *Dompl. 1, tel. 069/1337–6148. Dommuseum DM 4/€2. Church Mon.–Thurs. and Sat. 9–noon and 2:30–6; Fri. and Sun. 2:30–6 (closes at 5 in winter); Dommuseum Tues.–Fri. 10–5, weekends 11–5.*

⓲ KARMELITERKLOSTER (Carmelite Monastery). Secularized in 1803, the church and adjacent buildings were renovated in the 1980s and now contain the **Museum für Vor- und Frühgeschichte** (Museum of Prehistory and Early History). The **main cloister** (free; weekdays 8:30–5, weekends 10–5) displays the largest religious fresco north of the Alps, a 16th-century representation of Christ's birth and death by Jörg Ratgeb. *Karmeliterg. 1, tel. 069/2123–5896. Museum DM 8/€4; free Wed. Museum Tues. and Thurs.–Sun. 10–5, Wed. 10–8.*

⓼ KATHARINENKIRCHE (St. Catherine's Church). This house of worship, the first independent Protestant church in Gothic style, was originally built between 1678 and 1681 and restored after destruction in World War II. The church it replaced on this site, dating from 1343, was the setting of the first Protestant sermon preached in Frankfurt, in 1522. Goethe was confirmed here. Step inside to see the simple, postwar stained glass. *An der Hauptwache. Weekdays 2–6.*

⑯ LEONHARDSKIRCHE (St. Leonard's Church). Begun in the Romanesque style and continued in the late-Gothic style, this beautifully preserved church contains five naves, two 13th-century Romanesque arches, and 15th-century stained glass. Its "pendant," or hanging, vaulting was already a major Frankfurt tourist attraction in the 17th century. *Am Leonhardstor and Untermainkai. Tues.–Sun. 10–noon and 3–6.*

❻ LIEBFRAUENKIRCHE (Church of Our Lady). Dating from the 14th century, this late-Gothic church still has a fine tympanum relief over the south door and ornate rococo wood carvings inside. Outside is a delightful rococo fountain. *Liebfrauenberg 3. Daily 7–7, except during services.*

MESSEGELÄNDE (Fairgrounds). Also called the Congress Center, this huge complex is Europe's busiest trade-fair center and is constantly booked with congresses, conferences, and seminars. Important international trade fairs showcase the latest books, cars, fashion, technology, and consumer goods. In addition to the two major fairs in spring and fall, the center schedules the September automobile show in odd-numbered years, the Fur Fair at Easter, and the International Book Fair in the fall. *Ludwig-Erhard-Anlage 1, tel. 069/75750, www.messe-frankfurt.de.*

⑫ MUSEUM FÜR MODERNE KUNST (Museum of Modern Art). Austrian architect Hans Hollein designed this distinctive building shaped like a wedge of cake. The collection features American pop art and works by such German artists as Gerhard Richter and Joseph Beuys. *Domstr. 10, tel. 069/2123–0447. DM 10/€5. Tues. and Thurs.–Sun. 10–5, Wed. 10–8.*

⑳ NATURKUNDEMUSEUM SENCKENBERG (Senckenberg Natural History Museum). An important collection of fossils, animals, plants, and geological exhibits is upstaged by the famous diplodocus dinosaur, imported from New York—the only complete specimen of its kind in Europe. Many of the exhibits on prehistoric animals have been designed with children in mind, and there is a whole series of dioramas in which stuffed animals are presented. *Senckenberganlage 25, tel. 069/75420, www.senckenberg.uni-frankfurt.de. DM 7/€3.50. Mon., Tues., Thurs., and Fri. 9–5, Wed. 9–8, weekends 9–6.*

❸ NIKOLAIKIRCHE (St. Nicholas Church). This small red-sandstone church was built in the late 13th century as the court chapel for emperors of the Holy Roman Empire. Try to time your visit to coincide with the chimes of the carillon, which rings out three times a day, at 9, noon, and 5. *South side of Römerberg. Oct.–Mar., daily 10–6; Apr.–Sept., daily 10–8.*

🖐 ㉒ PALMENGARTEN UND BOTANISCHER GARTEN (Tropical Garden and Botanical Gardens). A splendid cluster of tropical and semitropical greenhouses contains a wide variety of flora, including cacti, orchids, and palms. The surrounding park has many recreational facilities: a little lake where you can rent rowboats, a play area for children, and a wading pool. Between the Palmengarten and the adjoining Grüneburgpark, the botanical gardens have a wide assortment of ornamental and rare plants from around the world. Special collections include a 2½-acre rock garden and rose and rhododendron gardens. During most of the year there are flower shows and exhibitions; in summer, concerts are held in an outdoor music pavilion. *Siesmayerstr. 63, tel. 069/2123–3939. DM 7/€3.50. Mar.–Oct., daily 9–6; Nov.–Jan., daily 9–4; Feb., daily 9–5.*

❺ PAULSKIRCHE (St. Paul's Church). This church was the site of the first all-German parliament in 1848. The parliament convened for only a year, having achieved little more than offering the Prussian king the crown of Germany. Today the church, which has been secularized and not very tastefully restored, remains a symbol of German democracy and is used mainly for ceremonies. The

German Book Dealers' annual Peace Prize is awarded in the hall, as is the Goethe Prize. *Paulspl. Daily 10–5.*

❷ RÖMER (City Hall). Three separate patrician structures make up the Römer. From left to right, they are the Alt-Limpurg, Zum Römer (from which the entire structure takes its name), and the Löwenstein. The mercantile-minded Frankfurt burghers used the complex not only for political and ceremonial purposes but also for trade fairs and other commercial ventures. Its gabled Gothic facade with an ornate balcony is widely known as the city's official emblem.

The most important events to take place in the Römer were festivities celebrating the coronations of Holy Roman Emperors. These were first held in 1562 in the glittering **Kaisersaal** (Imperial Hall), last used in 1792 to celebrate the election of Francis II, who would later be forced to abdicate by Napoléon. In 1765, at the banquet following the coronation of Joseph II, the 16-year-old Goethe posed as a waiter so as to get a first-hand look at the ceremonies, which he describes vividly in his autobiography *Dichtung und Wahrheit (Poetry and Truth).* When no official business is scheduled, you can admire the full-length 19th-century portraits of the 52 emperors of the Holy Roman Empire, which line the walls of the reconstructed banquet hall. *West side of Römerberg, tel. 069/2123–4814. DM 3/€1.50. Daily 10–1 and 2–5. Closed during official functions.*

❶ RÖMERBERG. This square north of the Main River, lovingly restored after wartime bomb damage, is the historical focal point of the city. The Römer, the Nikolaikirche, the Historiches Museum, and the half-timber Ostzeile houses are all found here. The 16th-century Fountain of Justice stands in the center of the square. At the coronation of Emperor Matthias in 1612, wine flowed from the fountain instead of water. The practice has been revived by the city fathers on special occasions. *Between Braubachstr. and the Main River.*

⑭ SCHIRN KUNSTHALLE (Schirn Art Gallery). One of Frankfurt's most modern museums is devoted exclusively to changing exhibits of modern art and photography. Past shows have included a survey of the German symbolist movement (1870–1920), the works of a contemporary news photographer, and Polish landscapes of the 19th and 20th centuries. The museum stands opposite the Kaiserdom. *Am Römerberg 6a, tel. 069/299–8820, www.shirn.de. DM 10/€5–DM 14/€7, depending on exhibition. Tues. and Sun. 11–7, Wed.–Sat. 11–10.*

⑪ STAUFENMAUER (Staufen Wall). The Staufenmauer, dating from the 12th century, is one of the few surviving sections of the city's original fortifications. *Fahrg.*

☙ STRUWWELPETER-MUSEUM (Slovenly Peter Museum). This museum contains a collection of letters, sketches, and manuscripts by Dr. Heinrich Hoffmann, a Frankfurt physician and creator of the children's book *Struwwelpeter*, featuring the character frequently encountered as a puppet or doll in Frankfurt's shops. *Schirn am Römerberg, tel. 069/281–333. Free. Tues. and Thurs.–Sun. 11–5, Wed. 11–8.*

ZEIL. The heart of Frankfurt's shopping district is this ritzy pedestrian street, running east from Hauptwache square. City officials claim it's the country's busiest shopping street. The Zeil is also known as "the Golden Mile."

★ ☙ ⑩ ZOOLOGISCHER GARTEN (Zoo). Founded in 1858, this is one of the most important and attractive zoos in Europe, with many of the animals and birds living in natural environments. Its remarkable collection includes some 5,000 animals of 600 different species, a bears' castle, an exotarium (aquarium plus reptiles), and an aviary, reputedly the largest in Europe. Nocturnal creatures move about in a special section. The zoo has a restaurant and a café and presents afternoon concerts in summer. *Alfred-Brehm Pl. 16, tel. 069/2123–3727. DM 11/€5.50. Nov.–Mar., daily 9–5; Apr.–Oct., daily 9–7.*

SACHSENHAUSEN

★ The old quarter of Sachsenhausen, on the south bank of the Main River, has been sensitively preserved, and its cobblestone streets, half-timber houses, and beer gardens make it a very popular area to stroll. Sachsenhausen's two big attractions are the Museumufer (Museum Bank), which has seven museums almost next door to one another, and the famous *Apfelwein* (apple-wine or cider) taverns around the Rittergasse pedestrian area. A green pine wreath above a tavern's entrance tells passersby that a freshly pressed—and alcoholic—apple cider is on tap. You can eat well in these small inns, too. Formerly a separate village, Sachsenhausen is said to have been established by Charlemagne, who settled the Main's banks with a group of Saxon families in the 8th century. It was an important bridgehead for the crusader Knights of the Teutonic Order and officially became part of Frankfurt in 1318.

A Good Walk

The best place to begin is at the charming 17th-century villa housing the **Städtische Galerie Liebieghaus** ㉔, the westernmost of the museums. It has an internationally famous collection of classical, medieval, and Renaissance sculpture. From it you need only turn to your right and follow the riverside road, Schaumainkai, for about 2 km (1 mi), passing all the museums and winding up around the Rittergasse.

The other museums are strung out before you. The **Städelsches Kunstinstitut und Städtische Galerie** ㉕ houses one of the most significant art collections in Germany, and the **Museum für Kommunication** ㉖ displays postal coaches, ancient telephones that work, and a huge stamp collection. The **Deutsches Architekturmuseum** ㉗ traces building from Stone Age huts to high-rises. Film artifacts and classic film videos are featured at the **Deutsches Filmmuseum** ㉘. After this museum, you could take a break at an Apfelwein tavern on Schweizer Strasse. The next museum after the bridge is the

Museum für Völkerkunde ㉙, which holds ethnological artifacts from the Pacific, Indonesia, Africa, and America. Next comes a stunning collection of European and Asian applied art in the **Museum für Kunsthandwerk** ㉚. Continue down the river road (the name changes from Schaumainkai to Sachsenhäuser Ufer) to the **Kuhhirtenturm** ㉛, the only remaining element of Sachsenhausen's original fortifications.

Just beyond the first bridge carrying car traffic, follow Grosse Rittergasse to the right. You will immediately be in the heart of the Apfelwein district, which is especially lively on summer evenings when it becomes one big outdoor festival. Some of the apple-wine taverns and other watering places are also open weekday afternoons. The area has a distinctly medieval air, with narrow back alleys, quaint little inns, and quiet squares that escaped the modern developer. Yet it's also full of new shops, cafés, and bars thronging with people.

TIMING

Allow an hour and 15 minutes for the Städelsches Kunstinstitut and Städtische Galerie, and an hour for the Städtische Galerie Liebieghaus. You could spend at least 45 minutes in each of the other museums along the walk. At the end of the day relax in an apple-wine tavern.

What to See

㉗ **DEUTSCHES ARCHITEKTURMUSEUM** (German Architecture Museum). Created by German architect Oswald Mathias Ungers, this 19th-century villa contains an entirely modern interior. There are five floors of drawings, models, and audiovisual displays that chart the progress of architecture through the ages, as well as many special exhibits. *Schaumainkai 43, tel. 069/2123–8844. DM 8/€4. Tues.–Sun. 10–5, Wed. until 8.*

㉘ **DEUTSCHES FILMMUSEUM** (German Film Museum). Germany's first museum of cinematography houses an exciting collection of film artifacts. Visitors can view its collection of classic film

videos, and a theater in the basement has regular evening
screenings of every sort of film from avant-garde to Hungarian
to silent-era flicks. *Schaumainkai 41, tel. 069/2123–8830,
www.deutsches-filmmuseum.de. DM 5/€2.50. Tues., Thurs., Fri., and Sun.
10–5, Wed. 10–8, Sat. 2–8.*

NEED A
BREAK?
Two of Sachsenhausen's swingingest Apfelwein taverns are well
removed from the Rittergasse and handy to the Museumufer.
You'll find them adjacent to one another if you turn right on
Schweizer Strasse, just beyond the Deutsches Filmmuseum, and
walk five minutes. **Zum Gemalten Haus** (Schweizer Str. 67, tel.
069/614–559) will provide all the hard cider and Gemütlichkeit
you could want. **Zum Wagner** (Schweizer Str. 71, tel. 069/612–
565) so reeks with "Olde Sachsenhausen" schmaltz that it's
downright corny.

---

31 **KUHHIRTENTURM** (Cowherd's Tower). This is the last of nine
towers, built in the 15th century, that formed part of
Sachsenhausen's fortifications. The composer Paul Hindemith
lived in the tower from 1923 to 1927, while working at the Frankfurt
Opera. *Sachsenhäuser Ufer.*

26 **MUSEUM FÜR KOMMUNICATION** (Communications Museum).
The former Postal Museum has moved very much into the
electronic age. Now you can log onto the Internet, talk to one
another on picture telephones, and learn about glass-fiber
technology. This is in addition to the historical postal exhibitions,
including mail coaches, stamps, ancient dial telephones with their
clunky switching equipment, and a reconstructed 19th-century
post office. *Schaumainkai 53, tel. 069/60600. Free. Tues.–Fri. 9–5,
weekends 11–7.*

30 **MUSEUM FÜR KUNSTHANDWERK** (Museum of Decorative Arts).
More than 30,000 objects representing European and Asian
applied arts are exhibited in this museum designed by American
architect Richard Meier. The collection of furniture, glassware,

and porcelain has expanded to include Web sites, computers, and graphic design. *Schaumainkai 17, tel. 069/2123–4037. DM 8/€4; free Wed. Tues. and Thurs.–Sun. 10–5, Wed. 10–8.*

㉙ MUSEUM FÜR VOLKERKUNDE (Ethnology Museum). Exhibits depict the lifestyles and customs of aboriginal societies from around the world. The collection includes masks, ritual objects, and jewelry. *Schaumainkai 29, tel. 069/2123–1510. DM 6/€3; free Wed. Tues. and Thurs.–Sun. 10–5, Wed. 10–8.*

★ **㉕ STÄDELSCHES KUNSTINSTITUT UND STÄDTISCHE GALERIE** (Städel Art Institute and Municipal Gallery). Here you will find one of Germany's most important art collections, with paintings by Dürer, Vermeer, Rembrandt, Rubens, Monet, Renoir, and other masters. The section on German Expressionism is particularly strong, with representative works by Frankfurt artist Max Beckmann. *Schaumainkai 63, tel. 069/605–0980. DM 10/€5; free Wed. Tues. and Thurs.–Sun. 10–5, Wed. 10–8.*

★ **㉔ STÄDTISCHE GALERIE LIEBIEGHAUS** (Liebieg Municipal Museum of Sculpture). The sculpture collection here, representing some 5,000 years of art history, is considered one of the most important in Europe. From antiquity the collection includes a statue of a Sumarian functionary and a relief from the temple of Egyptian king Sahure (2455–2443 BC). From the Middle Ages there is an 11th-century Madonna and child from Trier, and from the Renaissance an altar relief by the noted Florentine sculptor Lucca della Robbia (1399–1482). Works such as the *Immaculata*, by Matthias Steinl (1688), represent the Baroque era. Some pieces are exhibited in the lovely gardens surrounding the house. *Schaumainkai 71, tel. 069/2123–8617. DM 8/€4. Tues. and Thurs.–Sun. 10–5, Wed. 10–8.*

Smart Sightseeings

Savvy travelers and others who take their sightseeing seriously have skills worth knowing about.

DON'T PLAN YOUR VISIT IN YOUR HOTEL ROOM Don't wait until you pull into town to decide how to spend your days. It's inevitable that there will be much more to see and do than you'll have time for: choose sights in advance.

ORGANIZE YOUR TOURING Note the places that most interest you on a map, and visit places that are near each other during the same morning or afternoon.

START THE DAY WELL EQUIPPED Leave your hotel in the morning with everything you need for the day—maps, medicines, extra film, your guidebook, rain gear, and another layer of clothing in case the weather turns cooler.

TOUR MUSEUMS EARLY If you're there when the doors open you'll have an intimate experience of the collection.

EASY DOES IT See museums in the mornings, when you're fresh, and visit sit-down attractions later on. Take breaks before you need them.

STRIKE UP A CONVERSATION Only curmudgeons don't respond to a smile and a polite request for information. Most people appreciate your interest in their home town. And your conversations may end up being your most vivid memories.

GET LOST When you do, you never know what you'll find—but you can count on it being memorable. Use your guidebook to help you get back on track. Build wandering-around time into every day.

QUIT BEFORE YOU'RE TIRED There's no point in seeing that one extra sight if you're too exhausted to enjoy it.

TAKE YOUR MOTHER'S ADVICE Go to the bathroom when you have the chance. You never know what lies ahead.

In This Chapter

eating out

FRANKFURT'S LOCAL CUISINE comes from the region's farm tradition. Pork ribs and chops, stewed beef, blood sausage, potato soup, and pancakes with bacon fulfill proverbs such as "better once full than twice hungry" and "you work the way you eat." The city's most famous contribution to the world's diet is the Frankfurter Würstchen—a thin smoked pork sausage—better known to Americans as the hot dog. Grüne Sosse is a thin cream sauce of herbs served with potatoes and hard-boiled eggs. The oddly named Handkäs mit Musik (hand cheese with music) consists of slices of cheese covered with raw onions, oil, and vinegar, served with bread and butter (an acquired taste for many). All these things are served in Sachsenhausen Apfelwein (apple-wine, or hard-cider) taverns such as Fichtekränzi and Zum Wagner. Apfelwein, or Ebbelwoi in the Frankfurt dialect, is poured from a distinctive gray stoneware pitcher, called a Bembel, into an equally distinctive, ribbed tumbler. Many international cuisines are represented in the financial hub of Europe. For vegetarians there's usually at least one meatless dish on a German menu, and substantial salads are popular, too (though often served with bacon).

CATEGORY	COST*
$$$$	over DM 45/€23
$$$	DM 35/€18–DM 45/€23
$$	DM 25/€13–DM 35/€18
$	under DM 25/€13

*per person for a main course at dinner

city center and sachsenhausen dining

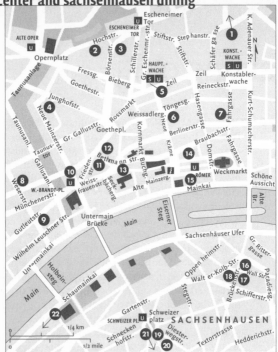

City Center

Aubergine, 1

Avocado Le Bistro, 2

Café Karin, 12

Chicago Meatpackers, 9

Dinea, 5

e-2 Energy Eatery, 8

Historix, 15

Kangaroo's, 3

Maggi Kochstudio Treff, 6

Maintower, 4

Mikuni, 7

Restaurant Français, 11

Sand, 10

Steinernes Haus, 14

Türkis, 13

Sachsenhausen

Bistrot 77, 22

Edelweiss, 21

Fichtekränzi, 17

Maingau Stuben, 18

Tandure, 16

Zum Wagner, 20

Zum Gemalten Haus, 19

CITY CENTER

$$$$ RESTAURANT FRANCAIS. Frankfurt's oldest hotel restaurant, in the Steigenberger Frankfurter Hof, offers sophisticated international fare with a French accent. The ornate green-and-gold dining room with Louis XIV furnishings and well-spaced tables is a perfect place to enjoy a business meal or the seven-course tasting menu, including breast of quail in lentil soup followed by duck supreme or baked turbo fillets in a mango-and-ginger sauce. *Bethmannstr. 33, tel. 069/215–138. Reservations essential. Jacket and tie. AE, DC, MC, V. Closed Sun., Mon., and 4 wks in July or Aug. No lunch Sat.*

$$$–$$$$ AVOCADO LE BISTRO. Graffiti artists have badly defaced its outer walls, but that doesn't hurt this very popular, romantic spot's reputation as one of Frankfurt's culinary institutions. The place is nearly as famous for its huge flower arrangements as it is for its superb bistro-style food and long list of wines. Chef Thierry Müller is the man behind the Mediterranean delicacies. *Hochstr. 27, tel. 069/292–867. AE, V. Closed Sun.*

$$$–$$$$ MIKUNI. A few paper lanterns and wall posters don't do much to offset the German furnishings, but the many Japanese patrons here vouch for the authenticity of the fare. The menu is in Japanese as well as German. Each arriving guest gets a hot towel, soup is drunk from the bowl, and even Germans seldom ask for a knife and fork to replace their chopsticks. Prices are more reasonable here than at other sushi bars. *Fahrg. 91–95, tel. 069/283–627. AE, MC.*

$–$$$ AUBERGINE. It's very small, with only six tables, and expensive. But the food, reminiscent of Chef Paolo Vargiu's native Sardinia, is excellent. The goose-liver terrine, leg of lamb fresh from the oven, and ragout of a whole lobster with broad beans are artfully placed on elegant Versace porcelain. *Alte Gasse 14, tel. 069/920–0780. Reservations essential. AE, DC, MC, V. Closed Sun.*

$–$$$ MAINTOWER. Atop the skyscraper that houses the Hessische
★ Landesbank, this popular restaurant cum café cum bar captures

an unbeatable view. Through 25-ft floor-to-ceiling windows, all of "Mainhattan" is at your feet. Prices are surprisingly reasonable, though you will have had to pay DM 6/3 per person just to take the elevator up. The cuisine is part global, part regional. It's hard to get a table for supper, though it's less of a problem for afternoon coffee or for an evening in the clouds at the bar. *Neue Mainzer Str. 52–58, tel. 069/3650–4770. AE, V.*

$–$$$ STEINERNES HAUS. Diners share long wooden tables beneath prints of Old Frankfurt and traditional clothing mounted on the walls. The house specialty is a rump steak brought to the table uncooked, with a heated rock tablet on which it is prepared. The beef broth is the perfect antidote to cold weather. The menu has other old German standards along with daily specials. Traditional fare popular with locals includes *Frankfurter Rippchen* (smoked pork) and *Zigeunerhackbraten* (spicy meat loaf). If you don't specify a *Kleines,* or small glass of beer, you'll automatically get a liter mug. *Braubachstr. 35, tel. 069/283–491. Reservations essential. MC, V.*

$–$$$ TÜRKIS. The name, which means "turquoise" (French for "Turkish"), says it all. The color itself dominates the setting, which is right out of an Ottoman palace. The traditionally prepared meat and fish dishes lean toward lamb and yogurt. A pianist plays every evening except Monday. *Bethmannstr. 4, tel. 069/296–694. AE, DC, MC, V.*

$–$$ CHICAGO MEATPACKERS. Americans who wonder if this place is what it claims to be should be glad to hear that it is the "official restaurant" (whatever that means) of the Frankfurt Galaxy American football team, the members of which are, with few exceptions, American gridiron types. If that doesn't convince you, the pitchers of beer, cocktails, all-you-can-eat spareribs, huge hamburgers, rock music blaring from loudspeakers, and model train running around the ceiling will. *Untermainanlage 8, tel. 069/231–659. AE, DC, MC, V.*

$–$$ KANGAROO'S. This very popular, Australia-theme restaurant has moved across the street to larger quarters, where its main dining room is glass-roofed and lush with greenery. The decor includes highway signs warning of kangaroos ahead. The adventurous will try the "Australia Platter," with kangaroo, crocodile, and emu meat (but Aussies, too, eat beef, chicken, and salads). Most people patronize this downtown restaurant for the food, but it's also a friendly place to gather for a Foster's beer and a chat. *Rahmhofstr. 2-4, tel. 069/131–0339. AE, DC, MC, V.*

$ CAFÉ KARIN. An understated café that attracts an interesting cross section of patrons, this is a great place to breakfast (only a few Marks or euros), to recover from a shopping spree, or to eat something healthy in preparation for a night out. Sample the goat-cheese salad or whole-grain ratatouille crepes. Cakes and baked goods come from the whole-grain bakery next door. There is a no-smoking section. *Grosser Hirschgraben 28, tel. 069/295–217. No credit cards.*

$ DINEA. Self-service restaurants are quite rare in Germany, but this brand-new chain outpost in the Kaufhof department store is one of the dividends of the department store's multi-million Mark renovation. The very extensive offerings—breakfast, salad bar, hearty German entrées like beef roulade, calorie-rich cakes—are inexpensive. With a separate entrance, the cafeteria is open well after the store has closed, and many evenings are given over to such entertainment as karaoke, piano nights, magic shows, and cocktail-mixing schools. *Zeil 116–126, tel. 069/2191–377. AE, DC, MC, V. Closed Sun. No dinner Sat.*

$ E-2 ENERGY EATERY. The power food offerings at this earthy place with color tones to match are billed as energy for the soul (spaghetti with a piquant sauce), for health (carrot salad), for the brain (potatoes with chestnuts), and for the nerves (turkey with vegetables). *Kaiserstr. 38, tel. 069/2380–2733. AE, DC, V. Closed Sun.*

$ HISTORIX. It goes without saying that Apfelwein is an important part of Frankfurt, and it's fitting that apple wine gets its own permanent exhibit in the Historisches Museum. Inside the museum, the Historix serves the beverage in Bembel pitchers and with all the typical food and accoutrements of the hard-cider business. The wall facing the street is one big plate-glass window, something you're not likely to find in a real tavern, but the decor more than makes up for this. Every inch of wall space covered with schmaltzy old pictures of the apple-wine scene, and historic Bembels are on display. The tables are overshadowed by a fake apple tree with huge fruit. *Saalg. 19, tel. 069/294–400. No credit cards. Closed Mon. No dinner weekends.*

$ MAGGI KOCHSTUDIO TREFF. The name Maggi is synonymous with soup. The century-old firm is primarily in the business of providing canned and dried soups and other foods for home consumption. But now it's trading on its reputation and serving the public's desire for light, inexpensive lunches and a cheap way of soothing between-meal hunger pangs. A Turkish lentil soup with sheep cheese and pita bread or a potato cream soup with sausage can hit the spot. Joining the bars in the burgeoning "happy hour" craze, Maggi discounts soups by DM 2/1 between 3 PM and 5 PM. *Neue Kräme 27, tel. 069/9139–9322. No credit cards. Closed Mon.*

$ SAND. The emphasis at this Lebanese restaurant is on lamb. The wide selection of hors d'oeuvres includes spiced vegetables, lamb sausages, sheep cheese, and yogurt. Sand also, unaccountably, has a bar where you can get skillfully made American cocktails, a rarity even in Frankfurt. Most of the tables are in a pleasant courtyard to the rear, which is covered in inclement weather with a translucent sliding roof. A pianist helps set the mood Friday and Saturday nights. *Kaiserstr. 25, tel. 069/2424–9440. AE, DC, MC, V. Closed Sun. No lunch Sat.*

WESTEND

$$$$ ERNO'S BISTRO. This tiny, unpretentious place in a quiet Westend
★ neighborhood looks like a poor candidate for "the best restaurant

in Germany." Yet that is what one French critic has called it, but that's just patriotism for you—after all, the French bistro's specialty, fish, is often flown in daily from France itself. Any critic will agree, however, that this old-timer with fresh, nouvelle preparations is one of the best restaurants in Frankfurt. It's closed weekends, during the Christmas and Easter seasons, and during much of the summer; in other words, when its clientele, the well-heeled elite of the business community, are unlikely to be in town. *Liebigstr. 15, tel. 069/721–997. Reservations essential. AE, DC, MC, V. Closed weekends and July–early Aug.*

$$$$ GARGANTUA. One of Frankfurt's most creative chefs, Klaus Trebes, who doubles as a food columnist, serves up new versions of German classics and French-accented dishes in a laid-back dining room decorated with contemporary art. His menu features such dishes as artichoke risotto with goose liver, lentil salad with stewed beef, and grilled dorade served on puréed white beans and pesto. One corner of the restaurant is reserved for those who only wish to sample the outstanding wine list. *Liebigstr. 47, tel. 069/720–718. AE, DC, MC, V. Closed Sun. No lunch Sat.*

$$$–$$$$ SURF N' TURF. Behind the Victorian facade that once housed the famous gourmet Humperdinck restaurant, surprised latecomers find a distinctly American steak house. The walls are lined with menus of famous U.S. examples of the genre and the menu covers basics like rib-eye and tenderloin steak, shrimp, and Dover sole. The beef comes exclusively from the United States. California wine is also served. *Gruneburgweg 95, tel. 069/722–122. AE, DC, MC, V. Closed Sun.*

$–$$$$ CAFÉ IM LITERATURHAUS. The Literaturhaus is part of the university library and naturally draws students, faculty, and anyone interested in literature. But you can get a lot more than a cup of coffee and a literary discussion. Austrian proprietor Franz Slunka and his Indian cook, Salwinder Singh, provide a mixture of European and international cuisines. There are lectures and

nordend, outer frankfurt, and westend dining

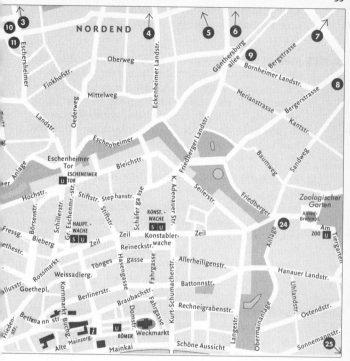

readings in the adjoining rooms of the Literaturhaus, though none in the café. *Bockenheimer Landstr. 102, tel. 069/745–550. MC, V. Closed Sat.*

$–$$$$ JEWEL OF INDIA. The elegant decor, gracious service, and delicious Indian-Pakistani food make the Jewel a good choice for lunch (it's just a couple of blocks from the trade-fair grounds). It's a lot calmer and quieter than the neighborhood's popular Italian restaurants. The chicken tandoori in saffron-yogurt marinade and lamb dishes such as *rogan josh* harmoniously blend spices and flavors without being overpowering. *Wilhelm-Hauff-Str. 5, tel. 069/752–375. AE, MC, V. No lunch Sat.*

$$$ KNOBLAUCH. Don't be turned off by the name of this intimate little place. It translates as "garlic," but the Alsatian menu, which is big on fowl, game, and fish dishes, isn't overly pungent. The tasty Alsatian blood sausage is prepared with apples and onions, and, of course, no restaurant featuring the cuisine of eastern France could omit quiche. Service is slow, and even though the humbly named restaurant is quite expensive, credit cards aren't accepted. *Staufenstr. 39, tel. 069/722–828. No credit cards. Closed weekends.*

$–$$ JOE PÉNAS. A hacienda atmosphere is created with rickety wooden tables and red candles that provide most of the lighting. The food is good: grilled meat and fish dishes are jazzed up with bananas, chilies, and corn. Even spiced turkey gets baked in a tortilla shell and topped with cheddar cheese. But the real fun is the flavored tequila—mint, vanilla, coffee—poured from an outsized decanter. There's an all-night happy hour whenever the moon is full. *Robert-Mayer-Str. 18, tel. 069/707–5156. AE, DC, V.*

$–$$ OMONIA. This cozy cellar locale offers the best Greek cuisine in town. Those with a good appetite should try the Omonia Platter, with lamb in several forms, plus Greek-style pasta and vegetables.

The place is popular and the tables are few, so make a reservation. *Vogtstr. 43, tel. 069/593–314. AE, DC, MC, V.*

$–$$ PIZZERIA ROMANELLA. Don't let the name and simple exterior fool you. This is a true *ristorante* with a very extensive menu of Italian fare. All the tables are full at supper time, when diners enjoy pastas and veal dishes. The pizza pies are good, but no better than elsewhere. *Wolfsgangstr. 84, tel. 069/596–1117. No credit cards. Closed Sat.*

$ CAFÉ LAUMER. The ambience of an old-time Viennese café, with a subdued decor and rear garden, is well preserved here. The place owes its literary tradition to Theodor Adorno, the philosopher and sociologist of the "Frankfurt School," who drank his daily coffee here. For fear of attracting more patrons than the often crowded café can handle, it isn't even listed in the phone book. In a compromise with café tradition, meals are also served, but the hours don't permit you to linger over a dinner. It's open for breakfast, lunch, and afternoon coffee, but closes at 7 PM. *Bockenheimer Landstr. 67, tel. 069/727912. DC, MC, V. No dinner.*

$ SANDWICHER. Even if you're just grabbing a sandwich, it doesn't have to be dull meal. Try a ciabatta with Parmesan cheese, ham, and marinated mozzarella, or a baguette with chicken breast or smoked salmon and avocado cream. There are sweets such as brownies to choose from as well. Between 4 PM and 6 PM, sandwiches are DM 1.50/.75 off. *Reuterweg 63, tel. 069/7103–4067. No credit cards. Closed weekends.*

NORDEND

$–$$ GROSSENWAHN. The Nordend is noted for its scene establishments, and this corner locale is the funkiest of them all, with bizarre artwork, thin strips of mirror, and a clientele that's definitely not from the banking community. The name translates as "Meglomania," which says it all. One whiff tells you that smoking is tolerated without restriction, and the menu spans the globe with German, Greek, Italian, and French contributions. *Lenaustr. 97, tel. 069/599–356. AE, MC, V.*

$–$$ HARVEY'S. This is very much the "in" place in Frankfurt today, the place to see and be seen. It first achieved its status as a gay and lesbian hangout, but the straight community is more and more attracted by the imaginative menu, good music, friendly atmosphere, and chameleon-like decor changes several times a year. The menu, too, changes regularly. Drinks are served with a baguette to nibble on and "breakfast" is available until 4 PM. *Bornheimer Landstr. 64, tel. 069/497–3032. No credit cards.*

$–$$ MONOLYA. This Turkish organic restaurant's motto, "bei uns haben Konservendosen Lokalverbot," loosely translates as "canned foods are banned from our premises." Everything on the vegetarian-oriented menu is homemade. Even the juices are freshly pressed and the draft beer is organic. The decor and music are distinctly Ottoman, as are the kabobs. *Habsburgallee 6a, tel. 069/494–0162. No credit cards.*

SACHSENHAUSEN

$$$$ BISTROT 77. The Mosbach brothers, sons of an Alsatian vintner whose wines they serve, offer outstanding food in spare bistro surroundings with plain walls and a tile floor. The menu is predominantly Alsatian with an accent on fresh vegetables and fine cuts of meat, such as lamb rib. An extravagant delicacy is grilled tuna fish with lobster medallions on white beans. The cheese wagon is rolled around at the end, and a Calvados or cognac tops things off nicely. *Ziegelhüttenweg 1–3, tel. 069/614–040. AE, MC, V. Closed Sun. No lunch Sat.*

$–$$$$ MAINGAU STUBEN. Chef Werner Döpfner himself greets you ★ and lights your candle at this very "in" restaurant. A polished clientele is drawn by the linen tablecloths, subdued lighting, and such nearly forgotten practices as carving the meat tableside. Chef Döpfner is one of Frankfurt's best, serving such contemporary dishes as seafood salad with scallops and lobster mousse, and rack of venison in a walnut crust. He also has a cellar full of rare German wines. *Schifferstr. 38, tel. 069/610–752. AE, MC, V. Closed Mon. No lunch Sat.*

$–$$ EDELWEISS. This place is full of homesick Austrians enjoying their native cuisine, including the genuine Wiener schnitzel and Kaiser Franz Josef's favorite, *Tafelspitze*, boiled beef with a chive sauce. Then there is the roast chicken with a salad made of "earth apples" (potatoes) and the beloved *Kaiserschmarrn*—egg pancakes with raisins, apples, cinnamon, and jam. The decor is rustically wooden within, and there is a pleasant terrace. *Schweizer Str. 96, tel. 069/619–696. AE, DC, MC, V.*

$–$$ FICHTEKRÄNZI. This is the real thing—a traditional apple-cider tavern in the heart of Sachsenhausen. In summer the courtyard is the place to be; in winter you sit in the noisy tavern proper at long tables with benches. It's often crowded, so if there isn't room when you arrive, order a glass of apple cider and hang around until someone leaves. Among the traditional cider-tavern dishes are *Rippchen* (smoked pork). *Wallstr. 5, tel. 069/612–778. No credit cards.*

$ TANDURE. The aroma of the clay oven—called a *tandure*—wafts through the dining room in this small Turkish restaurant decorated with Turkish carpeting and Anatolian handicrafts. As an appetizer you might want to try the *sigara böregi* (phyllo pastry stuffed with sheep cheese) or *imam bayildi* (stewed eggplant). Lamb, marinated and cooked in the tandure, is the house specialty. It's open until midnight. *Wallstr. 10, tel. 069/612–543. AE, V.*

$ ZUM GEMALTEN HAUS. This archetypal part of the Old Sachsenhausen Apfelwein scene is a favorite for young and old alike. The name means "At the Painted House," a reference to its rustic, oil-painted facade and stained-glass windows. Platters of meats and homemade sausages, juicy smoked pork chops, and snacks of soft cheese, vinegar, and onions are placed on long wooden tables. *Schweizer Str. 67, tel. 069/614–559. Reservations not accepted. No credit cards. Closed Mon. and Tues.*

$ ZUM WAGNER. ★ The kitchen here produces the same hearty German dishes offered at other apple-wine taverns, only better. Try the *Tafelspitz mit Frankfurter Grüner Sosse* (stewed beef with a sauce of green herbs), or come on Friday for fresh fish. Beer and wine are served as well as cider. This Sachsenhausen classic, with sepia-toned murals of merrymaking, succeeds in being touristy and traditional all at once. *Schweizer Str. 71, tel. 069/612–565. No credit cards.*

OUTER FRANKFURT

$$$$ WEIDEMANN. This half-timber country house is in a charming corner of Niederrad, a picturesque village now completely surrounded by Frankfurt. Chef Thomas Quecke presents a seafood-oriented menu that covers the map of Europe from Scandinavia (fjord salmon marinated in anise, mustard, and honey) to France (a *vol a vent* patty), to Italy (seafood ravioli). There's a delightful courtyard shaded by a chestnut tree for summer dining. Niederrad is on the south bank of the Main, to the east of Sachsenhausen. Weidemann can be reached by taking Tram 15 from the Hauptbahnhof to Schwarzwaldstrasse. Parking is no problem. *Kelsteracherstr. 66, tel. 069/675–996. AE, DC, MC, V. Closed Sun.*

$$$–$$$$ UNION CLUB RESTAURANT. The ordinary Frankfurt citizen no longer has to gaze at this elegant restaurant from the outside. Non-German correspondents could feast on steaks and tax-free booze courtesy of Uncle Sam's military when the villa, with an idyllic garden terrace, served as the Foreign Press Club after World War II. When it lost this "logistical support" it became a snooty private club, mainly for moneyed expatriates. It still carries on its high-toned tradition, with a menu leaning toward fish and game. *Am Leonhardsbrunn 12, tel. 069/703–033. AE, DC, MC, V. No dinner weekends.*

$$ ALTES ZOLLHAUS. Very good versions of traditional German specialties are served in this beautiful, 200-year-old half-timber house on the edge of town. Try a game dish. In summer you can eat in the beautiful garden. To get here, take Bus 30 from Konstablerwache to Heiligenstock, or drive out on Bundestrasse 521 in the direction of Bad Vilbel. *Friedberger Landstr. 531, tel. 069/ 472–707. AE, DC, MC, V. Closed Mon. No lunch except Sun.*

$–$$ ARCHE NOVA. This sunny establishment is a feature of Frankfurt's Ökohaus, which was built according to environmental principles (solar panels, catching rainwater, etc.). In keeping with the character of the place, it's more or less vegetarian with such dishes as a vegetable platter with feta cheese or a curry soup with grated coconut and banana. Much of what's served, even some of the beers, is organic. *Kasselerstr. 1a, tel. 069/707–5859. No credit cards.*

$–$$ GERBERMÜHLE. Many think this is the finest outdoor restaurant in the city. It's right on the bank of the Main in the Oberrad district to the east of Sachsenhausen, and can be reached on a pleasant, one-hour riverside hike from downtown. It's so old that Goethe, the city's favorite son, liked to patronize it. The menu features typical Frankfurt and German fare. *Deutschherrnufer 105, tel. 069/ 965–2290. AE, V.*

$–$$ KING CREOLE. The good times roll at the closest thing to a French Quarter restaurant Frankfurt will ever see. Dine on New Orleans staples like jambalaya or Cajun popcorn (crisply fried shrimp with a piquant sauce) in the pleasant garden, or inside to piped-in jazz. *Eckenheimer Landstr. 346, tel. 069/542–172. AE, DC, MC, V.*

$–$$ WÄLDCHES. This is Frankfurt's busiest brewpub, in a countrified
★ location nevertheless handy to a transit station, and a favorite stop for bikers and hikers. By noon on pleasant summer Sundays, the big beer garden can be standing-room only. The home-brewed light and dark beers go nicely with the largely German cuisine, which is substantial but not stodgy. If you like the beer you can

take some of it with you in an old-fashioned bottle with a wired porcelain stopper. *Am Ginnheimer Wäldchen 8, tel. 069/520–522. No credit cards.*

$–$$ ZUM RAD. Named for the huge wagon wheel (*Rad*) that decorates it, this Apfelwein tavern is in the small, village-like district of Seckbach, off the northeastern edge of the city. Outside tables are shaded by chestnut trees in a large courtyard. The typically Hessian cuisine includes such dishes as *Ochsenbrust* (brisket of beef) and Handkäs mit Musik. *Leonhardsg. 2, Seckbach, tel. 069/479–128. No credit cards. Closed Tues.*

$ ABESSINIA. Dishes at this Ethiopian restaurant are meant to be shared. Pull off a piece of thin, spongy *injera* bread to sop up the spicy, predominantly vegetarian, stew-like dishes (knives and forks are available if you insist). You can wash it down with beer or juices from passion fruit, pineapple, and banana. The decor is stridently African, with lots of greenery, painted elephants and zebras, and stuffed birds hanging from the ceiling. *Pfingstweidstr. 2, tel. 069/439–108. No credit cards.*

$ DR. FLOTTE. This smoky tavern is right out of another era, with high ceilings, arched windows, and a collection of early appliances, including radios and sewing machines. It's in the middle of the university district, and students join the 80-year-old ladies quaffing beer. The varied, largely German cuisine is quite affordable. *Gräfstr. 87, tel. 069/704–595. No credit cards.*

$ MOMBERGER. This merry spot in the outlying district of Heddernheim is one of the many typical apple-wine locales that does not happen to be located in Sachsenhausen. It's a picturebook setting with apple wine from wooden vats, generous platters of smoked meats, and centuries-old tradition. Portions and prices are also somewhat reminiscent of the old days. *Alt Heddernheim 13, tel. 069/576–666. No credit cards. Closed Sat.*

Eating Well is the Best Revenge

Eating out is a major part of every travel experience. It's a chance to explore flavors you don't find at home. And often the walking you do on vacation means that you can dig in without guilt.

START AT THE TOP By all means take in a really good restaurant or two while you're on the road. A trip is a time to kick back and savor the pleasures of the palate. Read up on the culinary scene before you leave home. Check out representative menus on the Web—some chefs have gone electronic. And ask friends who have just come back. Then reserve a table as far in advance as you can, remembering that the best establishments book up months in advance. Remember that some good restaurants require you to reconfirm the day before or the day of your meal. Then again, some really good places will call you, so make sure to leave a number where you can be reached.

ADVENTURES IN EATING A trip is the perfect opportunity to try food you can't get at home. So leave yourself open to try an ethnic food that's not represented where you live or to eat fruits and vegetables you've never heard of. One of them may become your next favorite food.

BEYOND GUIDEBOOKS You can rely on the restaurants you find in these pages. But also look for restaurants on your own. When you're ready for lunch, ask people you meet where they eat. Look for tiny holes-in-the-wall with a loyal following. Find out about local chains whose fame rests upon a single memorable dish. There's hardly a food-lover who doesn't relish the chance to share a favorite place. It's fun to come up with your own special find—and asking about food is a great way to start a conversation.

SAMPLE LOCAL FLAVORS Do check out the specialties. Is there a special brand of ice cream or a special dish that you simply must try?

HAVE A PICNIC Every so often eat al fresco. Grocery shopping gives you a whole different view of a place.

In This Chapter

shopping

THERE IS LITTLE that can't be bought in Frankfurt. The main downtown shopping area is centered on the Hauptwache, and within a half-mile of it you can find clothing, furniture, electronics, books, food and drink, health and beauty items, and more. Three of the city's poshest shopping streets, the Zeil, Goethe Strasse, and Grosse Bockenheimer Strasse, branch off from the Hauptwache, and beneath it is an underground shopping mall. For more casual shopping, there's a big weekly flea market across the Main River to the south.

It pays to watch for the two annual sales; the Winter-Schlussverkauf and the Sommer-Schlussverkauf. The bargains you find at these can be downright unbelievable. By law these sales begin on the first Saturday of January and July and run until the second Saturday following.

Stores may be open weekdays from 6 AM to 8 PM and Saturday from 6 AM to 4 PM. They must remain closed on Sunday, and the 4 PM closing on Saturday makes for crowds of people trying to get their odds and ends secured before another week passes them by. The airport doubles as a mall whose stores are allowed to ignore the otherwise strict closing hours.

SHOPPING DISTRICTS

The tree-shaded pedestrian zone of the **Zeil** is claimed to be the richest shop-'til-you-drop mile in Germany. Other cities ask where Frankfurt gets the figures to prove the claim, but there is no doubt that the Zeil, between the Hauptwache and Konstablerwache stations, is incredible for its variety of department and specialty stores.

The Zeil is only the centerpiece of the downtown shopping area. West of the Hauptwache are two parallel and highly regarded streets. One is the luxurious **Goethestrasse,** lined with boutiques, art galleries, jewelry stores, and antiques shops. The other is **Grosse Bockenheimer Strasse,** better known as the Fressgasse ("Pig-Out Alley"). Cafés, restaurants, an arcade, and, especially, pricey food stores line the street, tempting gourmands with everything from crumbly cheeses and smoked fish to vintage wines and chocolate creams.

The Zeil area abounds in arcades. The moderately priced **Zeilgallerie** (Zeil 112–114, tel. 069/9207–3414) has 56 shops and an IMAX theater. The **Schillerpassage** (Rahmhofstr. 2) is strong on men's and women's fashion boutiques. The subway station beneath the **Hauptwache** also doubles as a vast underground mall.

Near the cathedral and the river you'll find art and antiques shops on **Braubachstrasse, Fahrgasse,** and **Weckmarkt.**

DEPARTMENT STORES AND ARCADES

Two department stores, Galerie Kaufhof and Hertie, have competed on the Zeil for many years, offering much in the way of clothing, furnishings, electronics, and foodstuffs. After seven months as a chaotic building site, which drove many customers down the Zeil to other stores, the Kaufhof has grandly rechristened itself the **Galerie Kaufhof** (Zeil 116–126, tel. 060/21910). Shoppers are drawn by an array of up-to-date retailing practices, such as the shop-in-shop concept for fashions and touch screens that describe products. (One tells you what wines at what temperature go with what food.) The renovation has also produced a much-improved top-floor restaurant with a striking view.

Hertie (Zeil 90, tel. 069/929–050) is the equal of any other department store on the Zeil with its array of clothing, furnishings, and electronics, and beats them all with its basement Hertie Gourmet food store. In departments like Neptune's Kingdom (where they fillet the fresh fish before your eyes), Steakpoint, and Sushi Circle, and a cellar with 800 varieties of wine, customers find the most extensive food and drink selection in a city known for its culinary offerings.

SPECIALTY SHOPS

CLOTHING STORES

Men shop at **Bailly & Diehl** (Börsenstr. 2–4, tel. 069/20845) for well-known labels.

All the top women's designers are represented in Inge Winterberg's collection at **Class-X** (Börsenstr. 7-11, tel. 069/131–0853). The store carries bags from Coccinelle, shoes from Free Lance, and jewelry from Rio Berlin. Tailors can provide a garment in another color or fabric if the lady likes, but the styles can't be altered.

Cravatterie Frankfurt (Goethestr. 37, tel. 069/284–763) specializes in neckties and scarves from all the top designers— Dior, Yves St. Laurent, Versace. Prices are what you would expect. Styles range from classic to trendy, and the main thrust is Italian. There are also umbrellas, and orders are taken for Italian shoes.

Peek & Cloppenburg (Zeil 71–75, tel. 069/298–950) is a huge, well-organized clothing store where men and women can find what they need for everything from the dance club to the office to the gym. Clothes range from the easily affordable to eyebrow-raising, world-renown labels.

Women shop at **Pfüller Modehaus** (Goethestr. 15–17, tel. 069/1337–8070) for the wide range of merchandise on three floors, from classic to trendy, from lingerie to overcoats, from hats to stockings. Louis Féraud, Strenesse, René Lezard, and Roberto Cavalli are just a few of the many labels stocked.

Prenatal (An der Hauptwache 7, tel. 069/288–001) sells a comprehensive collection of baby and maternity clothes.

HOME FURNISHINGS

Cri-Cri (Rossmarkt 13, tel. 069/131–00606) has three floors dedicated to furniture and the decorative arts. There are drapes and bed linens, antique-looking wardrobes, and Japanese-style paper lanterns. Cri-cri also carries a selection of teas, coffees, and Italian wines—and offers samples.

Das Depot (Zeil 121, tel. 069/2199–7585) provides whatever you need around the house, from terra-cotta vases and candlesticks to artificial flowers, colored sand, and widgets to satisfy the do-it-yourselfer. Environmentalists are assured that the teak furniture comes only from tree plantations.

FLEA MARKETS

Sachsenhausen's flea market takes place on Saturday from 8 to 2, between **Dürerstrasse** and the **Eiserner Steg**. It used to be known for a wide range of used merchandise, sometimes antiques, sometimes junk, but purveyors of the cheap seem to have taken over. Get there early for the bargains. The better-quality stuff gets snapped up quickly. Shopping success or no, the market can be fun browsing.

FOOD AND DRINK

The pastry shop **Konditorei Lochner** (Kalbächerg. 10, tel. 069/
920–7320) has such local delicacies as *Bethmännchen und Brenten*
(marzipan cookies) or *Frankfurter Kranz* (a kind of creamy cake).
All types of sweets and pastries are found at the café **Laumer**
(Bockenheimer Landstr. 67, tel. 069/727–912).

Don't be fooled by the cramped size of **Perkel & Partner**
(Kaiserstr. 31-33, tel. 069/234–413); it can come up with wines
from the world over. It also carries cigars and spirits.

Weinhandlung Dr. Teufel (Kleiner Hirschgraben 4, tel. 069/
283–236) is as good a wine shop as any for popular vintages, but
the best place in town for diversity. There's also a complete line
of glasses, carafes, corkscrews, and other accessories, and
books on all aspects of viticulture.

GIFT IDEAS

Cold, hard cash, not souvenirs, is what springs to mind when in
Germany's financial capital. Frankfurt does produce fine
porcelain, though, and it can be bought at the **Höchster
Porzellan Manufaktur,** in the suburb of Höchst (☞ Side Trips).

One thing typical of Frankfurt is its Apfelwein (hard cider). You
can get a bottle of it at any grocery store, but more enduring
souvenirs would be the *Bembel* (pitchers) and glasses that are
equally a part of the Apfelwein tradition. The blue stoneware
Bembel have a fat belly, and the glasses are ribbed to give them
"traction" (in the old days this was good for preventing the
glass from slipping from greasy hands). **Lorey** (Schillerstr. 16,
tel. 069/299–950) sells apple-wine pitchers and glasses along
with a wide assortment of tableware and other household
goods.

A famous children's book in Germany, *Struwwelpeter* (*Slovenly
Peter*), was the work of a Frankfurt doctor, Heinrich Hoffmann.

Clothing Size Conversion Chart

Women's Clothing

US	UK	EUR
4	6	34
6	8	36
8	10	38
10	12	40
12	14	42

Women's Shoes

US	UK	EUR
5	3	36
6	4	37
7	5	38
8	6	39
9	7	40

Men's Suits

US	UK	EUR
34	34	44
36	36	46
38	38	48
40	40	50
42	42	52
44	44	54
46	46	56

Men's Shirts

US	UK	EUR
14 ½	14 ½	37
15	15	38
15 ½	15 ½	39
16	16	41
16 ½	16 ½	42
17	17	43
17 ½	17 ½	44

Men's Shoes

US	UK	EUR
7	6	39 ½
8	7	41
9	8	42
10	9	43
11	10	44 ½
12	11	46

He wrote the poems and drew the rather amateurish pictures in 1844 just to warn his own children of the dire consequences of being naughty. He did not originally intend to publish the book, but the response of his kids and his friends convinced him he had a gem on his hands. The book has seen several English translations; one by Mark Twain no less! The **Struwwelpeter-Museum** (Schirm am Römerberg, tel. 069/281–333) has copies of some of them, including one with the German and Mark Twain versions on facing pages. The museum's gift shop also has cups, pins, and coloring books.

An edible gift you can take home is the frankfurter sausage, which gave America one of its favorite sandwiches. The hot dog, on a long roll, made its first appearance at the 1893 World's Columbian Exhibition in Chicago, and this sausage, sent over in cans from Frankfurt, was the basic ingredient. It's still available in cans. Try **Plöger** on the Fressgasse (Grosse Bockenheimer Str. 30, tel. 069/138–7110). One taste of this high-quality smoked sausage will convince you that American imitations resemble the true frankfurter only in size and shape.

In This Chapter

outdoor activities and sports

FRANKFURT IS FULL OF PARKS and other green oases where you can breathe easier once the summer smog sets in. A semicircle of parkland surrounds the downtown. South of the city, the huge, 4,000-acre Städtwald makes Frankfurt one of Germany's most forested metropolises. The forest has innumerable paths and trails, bird sanctuaries, impressive sports stadiums, and a number of good restaurants. The Waldlehrpfad trail there leads past a series of rare trees, each identified by a small sign. The Oberschweinstiege stop on streetcar Line 14 is right in the middle of the park. Alternately, you can take Bus 36 from Konstablerwache to Hainerweg.

The **Taunus Hills** are a great getaway for Frankfurters, and public transportation gets you there without hassle. Take U-Bahn 3 to Hohemark. In the Seckbach district, northeast of the city, Frankfurters hike the 590-ft **Lohrberg Hill.** The climb rewards you with a fabulous view of the town and the Taunus, Spessart, and Odenwald hills. Along the way you'll also see the last remaining vineyard within the Frankfurt city limits, the Seckbach Vineyard. Take the U-Bahn 4 to Seckbacher Landstrasse, then Bus 43 to Draisbornstrasse.

PARTICIPANT SPORTS

BIKING

Frankfurt's outer parks and forests are terrific for recreational biking. In summer you can rent bikes at the **Goetheturm** (Goethe Tower; tel. 069/49111), on the northern edge of the Stadtwald.

BOWLING

Bowling and Kegelncenter Rebstock (Am Römerhof 13, tel. 069/702–070) has 30 lanes for bowling and nine lanes for *Kegeln*, the old, German-style nine-pin bowling that is rapidly being driven out of existence by the American version. It also has billiard tables and a bar-restaurant. Lanes cost DM 4/€2 before 7 PM, DM 5.50/€2.75 afterward, and shoe rental is DM 2/€1. Reservations are highly advisable on Friday and Saturday.

FITNESS CENTERS

Near the central Hauptwache, the **Fitness Company** (Zeil 109, tel. 069/9637–3100) has everything anyone needs to work out. There are more than 60 aerobics and other classes and 150 different fitness machines, from Nautilus to StairMaster. English is spoken. A day's training costs DM 35/€18. The **Fitness Center für Frauen** (Fitness Center for Women; Studio 1, Grosse Gallusstr. 1, tel. 069/9637–3500) is exclusively for women and costs DM 35/€18 per day.

GOLF

There's an 18-hole course in the city, **Frankfurter Golfclub** (Golfstr. 41, tel. 069/66–2317). **Waldstadion Frankfurt** (Mörfelder Landstr. 362, tel. 069/6980–4222) has a nine-hole course.

ICE SKATING

The **Eissporthalle** (Am Bornheimer Hang 4, tel. 069/2123–0810), near the Ostpark, provides indoor ice-skating on two rinks and a 400-meter track from November to April.

JOGGING

The banks of the Main River are good places to jog, and to avoid retracing your steps you can always cross a bridge and return down the opposite side. In the city center, **Grüneberg Park** is 2 km (1 mi) around, with a *Trimm Dich* (get fit) exercise facility in the northeast corner. The **Anlagenring**, a park following the line of the old city walls around the city, is also a popular route. For a vigorous forest run, go to the Stadtwald or the Taunus hills.

ROLLERBLADING

Skilled bladers gather at 8:30 PM Tuesday night, March to October, for a 2½-hour glide through the city. This 20- to 30-km (12- to 18-mi) race always starts at the Deutschherrenufer on the Main River in Sachsenhausen, but follows different routes. You can also blade anytime along the paved paths along the Main.

SWIMMING

Incredible as it may seem, people used to swim off the banks of the Main. Pictures from as recent as the 1930s show happy crowds splashing in a roped-off area. That day is long gone (you'd probably dissolve), but there are a number of indoor and outdoor pools. The often-crowded **Brentanobad** (Rödelheimer Parkweg, tel. 069/2123–9020) is an outdoor pool surrounded by lawns and old trees. The leisure center **Rebstockbad** (August-Euler-Str. 7, tel. 069/708–078) has an indoor pool, a pool with a wave machine and palm-fringed beach, and an outdoor pool with giant water chutes. The **Stadionbad** (Morfelder Landstr. 362, tel. 069/678–040) has an outdoor pool, a giant water chute, a solarium, and exercise lawns. For everything from "adventure pools" and bowling to a sauna and fitness center, head to the **Titus Therme** (Walter-Möller-Pl. 2, tel. 069/958–050).

TENNIS
Europa Tennis & Squash Park (Ginheimer Landstr. 49, tel. 069/532–040) has eight courts. **Waldstadion** (Mörfelder Landstr. 362, tel. 069/678–7346) has three indoor and five outdoor courts. Book in advance.

SPECTATOR SPORTS

Many major sporting events take place in the complex, **Waldstdion Frankfurt** (Mörfelder Landstr. 362, tel. 069/698–040).

AMERICAN FOOTBALL
There's plenty of opportunity in Frankfurt for those who like to take their sports sitting down. Believe it or not, the city has its own American professional football team, the **Frankfurt Galaxy** (Westerbachstr. 47, tel. 0180/526–6216). It belongs to the World League of American Football, along with such other European teams as London and Barcelona. The Galaxy, most of whose players come from the States, have done well in the past, winning the league's cup in 1995 and 1999. Though they have fallen on leaner times of late, fans still regularly fill the large Waldstadion for home games. That makes it the only profitable team in the WLAF, which is partly owned by the NFL. Games are played between April and June.

BASKETBALL
The basketball team the **Skyliners** (Silostr. 46, Höchst, tel. 069/3083–8864) is sponsored by Opel, the automotive firm, and plays its games at the Ballsporthalle in Höchst. Though there are 14 teams in the S. Oliver Basketball Bundesliga, the Skyliners

managed to get into the semifinals of the 2000 championships. Its rules permit only two Americans on the floor at any time.

ICE HOCKEY

Frankfurt's **Lions** (Am Bornheimer Hang 4, tel. 069/4058–840) is one of 16 teams in the Deutsche Eishockey Liga, in which it hasn't been overly successful so far. Sponsored by the firm of Mannesmann-Arcor, it plays its games at the Eissporthalle, near the Ostpark, and has a number of American players.

SOCCER

Sharing the Waldstadion with the Galaxy football team is Frankfurt's beloved soccer team, the **Eintracht** (Am Erlenbruch 25, tel. 01805/743–1899). Fans attend its home games with the knowledge that this once-glorious team now has no way to go but up. A women's soccer team, the **1. FFC Frankfurt** (Brentanobad, Rödelheimer Parkweg, tel. 06074/82840), frequently holds first place in the National League and has shown the Eintracht gentlemen how soccer ought to be played. Games are played at the Brentanobad.

In This Chapter

nightlife and the arts

FRANKFURT WAS A REAL PIONEER in the German jazz scene, and has also, more recently, done much for the development of techno music. Jazz musicians make the rounds from smoky backstreet cafés all the way to the Old Opera House, and in the fall the German Jazz Festival takes place in conjunction with the Music Fair. The Frankfurter Jazzkeller has been a mecca for German jazz fans for decades.

THE ARTS

Frankfurt has the largest budget for cultural affairs of any city in the country. The Städtische Bühnen—municipal theaters, including the city's opera company—are the prime stages. Frankfurt has what is probably the most lavish theater in the country, the Alte Oper, a magnificently ornate 19th-century opera house. The building is no longer used for opera, but serves as a multipurpose hall for pop and classical concerts and dance performances.

Theater tickets can be purchased from theater box offices, the tourist office at Römerberg 27, and the following agencies. **Frankfurt Ticket GmbH** (Hauptwache Passage, tel. 069/134–0400) is one of the best ticket agencies. **Ticket Direct** (Ottostr. 3a tel. 069/201–156) is outside the main train station. **Kartenvorverkauf GmbH** (Liebfrauenberg 52–54, tel. 069/920–300) is just south of the Hauptwache. The **Hertie department store** (Zeil 90, tel. 069/294–848) has its own ticket office.

BALLET, CONCERTS, AND OPERA

The most glamorous venue for classical music concerts is the **Alte Oper** (Opernpl., tel. 069/134–0400). Tickets to performances can range from DM 20/10 to nearly DM 300/154. The **Frankfurt Opera** (Städtische Bühnen, Untermainanlage 11, tel. 069/2123–7999) has made a name for itself as a company specializing in dramatic artistry. Sharing the same venue as the Frankfurt Opera, the world-renowned **Frankfurt Ballet** (Städtische Bühnen, Untermainanlage 11, tel. 069/2123–7319) is under the modern-thinking direction of American William Forsythe.

The **Festhalle** (Ludwig-Erhard-Anlage 1, tel. 069/7575–6404), on the fairgrounds, hosts rock concerts, horse shows, ice shows, sporting events, and other large-scale spectaculars.

The city is also the home of the Radio-Sinfonie-Orchester Frankfurt, part of Hessischer Rundfunk. It performs regularly in the 850-seat **Kammermusiksaal** (Bertramstr. 8, tel. 069/550–123), part of the broadcasting operation's campus-like facilities.

FILM

If dialogue in German will fly over your head, English-language movies are still an option since they're not hard to find here. In the papers, look for the letter "O" in an abbreviation, as in "OV" (Originalversion), "OF" (Originalfassung), or "OmU" (Original mit Untertiteln, meaning captions). If you also see the abbreviation "Engl.," you're all set—although just because a film's title is in English don't assume that the soundtrack will be as well. When a film is "original" it's usually in English, but you can't count on it. The country of a film's origin is also usually given, such as "USA" or "GB." Combination restaurant-and-cinema establishments have won audiences not so much for the food as for the convenience, but they rarely show films in English.

The multiplex theater **Turm-Palast** (Grosse Eschersheimer Str. 20, tel. 069/281–787) presents nothing but English-language films on its eight screens, usually the latest releases. The **Film Museum** (Schaumainkai 41, tel. 069/2123–8830) shows about half its films in English. There are three screenings daily of classic, avant-garde, esoteric, and other films in its basement Kommunales Kino.

At the **IMAX** (Zeil 112–114, tel. 069/1338–4830), where you are entirely surrounded by a gigantic screen, the little dialogue there is is in German, but the thrills are the spectacles of Mount Everest, the Serengeti, and Earth, and a stomach-turning plunge down a ski slope.

Mal Seh'n (Adlerflychtstr. 6h, tel. 069/597–0845), on the edge of the Nordend, a restaurant-and-theater combination; you can bring your drink from the restaurant into the theater, but not your food. At the restaurant-cum-cinema **Orefeo's Eben** (Hamburger Allee 45, tel. 069/7076–9100) you can take both a drink and finger food to your seat in the theater; stick with the simplest options on the menu.

THEATER

Theatrical productions in Frankfurt are nearly always in German, of course, or, in the case of the alternative Die Schmiere, in German dialect. For English-language productions, try the **English Theater** (Kaiserstr. 52, tel. 069/2423–1620). Under the talented direction of American Judith Rosenbauer, it puts on an array of musicals, thrillers, dramas, and comedy with British or American casts. The **Internationales Theater** (Hanauer Landstr. 5–7, tel. 069/499–0980) draws artists from far and wide, many of them English-speaking, to perform in their native languages.

The **Künstlerhaus Mouson Turm** (Waldschmidtstr. 4, tel. 069/4058–9520) is a cultural center that hosts a regular series of concerts of all kinds, as well as plays and exhibits. The repertoire at the municipally owned **Schauspielhaus** (Willy-Brandt-Pl., tel.

069/2123–7999) includes works by Sophocles, Goethe, Shakespeare, Brecht, and Beckett. For a zany theatrical experience, try **Die Schmiere** (Seckbächerg. 2, tel. 069/281–066), which offers trenchant satire and also calls itself, disarmingly, "the worst theater in the world." Renowned for international experimental productions, including dance theater and other forms of nonverbal drama, is the **Theater am Turm** (TAT; Bockenheimer Warte, tel. 069/2123–7999) in the Bockenheimer Depot, a former trolley barn.

NIGHTLIFE

Frankfurt at night is a city of stark contrasts. Old hippies and baby-faced counterculturalists, Turkish and Greek guest workers, people on pensions, chess players, exhibitionists, and loners all have their piece of the action. People from the banking world seek different amusements than the city's 40,000-plus students, but their paths cross in places like the cider taverns in Sachsenhausen and the gay bars of the Nordend. Sachsenhausen (Frankfurt's "Left Bank") is a good place to start for bars, clubs, and Apfelwein taverns. The ever-more-fashionable Nordend has an almost equal number of bars and clubs but fewer tourists. Frankfurt is one of Europe's leading cities for techno, the computer-generated music of ultrafast beats that's the anthem of German youth culture. A major trend at night spots is the "After Work" or "After Hours," happy hour with half-price drinks, lasting usually from 5 or 6 to 9 or 10 one weekday per week. Jimmy's has one every weeknight, the Opium on Tuesday, Monza and the Studio Bar on Wednesday, and the Galerie on Thursday. Most bars close somewhere between 2 AM and 4 AM.

APPLE WINE

The tables at the **Lorsbacher Tal** (Grosse Ritterg. 49, tel. 069/616–459), in a courtyard behind an Art Nouveau gate, are in special demand. It's a very typical Sachsenhausen apple-wine tavern. If you're one of those who go to an Apfelwein tavern for the atmosphere but not the sour apple wine, you'd better skip this one. It snobbishly refuses to serve beer.

BARS AND LOUNGES

Wagons and pushcarts decorate the cellar Irish pub **An Sibin** (Wallstr. 9, tel. 069/603–2159), presumably to remind you of the Emerald Isle's folksy character. Serious elbow lifting and heartfelt conversations take place in English, Gaelic, Hessian dialect, and German. There is live music most nights along with Guinness right out of the keg and some good pub grub. It's closed Sunday.

The tiny, cozy **Balalaika** (Dreikönigstr. 30, tel. 069/612–226), in Sachsenhausen, provides intimacy and live music without charging the fancy prices you'd expect at such a place. The secret is proprietress Anita Honis, a professional American singer from Harlem who usually gets out her acoustic guitar several times during an evening.

If you're seeking something soothing, sit down at **Casablanca Bar** (Parkhotel, Wiesenhüttenpl. 28, tel. 069/26970) and listen to the pianist. For a strong elixer, ask the bartender to shake up a "Tropica Girl" or "Humphrey's Special."

Like much of the Marriott Hotel it's in, the **Champion's Bar** (Hamburger Allee 2–10, tel. 069/7955–2463) is designed to make Americans feel at home. The wall is lined with jerseys, autographed helmets, and photographs of American athletes. The TV is tuned to baseball, American football, and basketball broadcasts, and the food leans to buffalo wings, potato skins, and hamburgers. Parties take place on American holidays like Halloween, Thanksgiving, and Valentine's Day.

Frankfurt teems with Irish pubs, but **Fox and Hound** (Niedenau 2, tel. 069/9720–2009) is the only *English* pub in town. The patrons, mainly British, come to watch constant satellite transmissions of the latest football (soccer to you Americans), rugby, and cricket matches, to enjoy the authentic pub grub (try the basket of chips), and to participate in the Sunday-night quiz for free drinks and cash prizes. It's a noisy bunch.

Jimmy's Bar (Friedrich-Ebert-Anlage 40, tel. 069/7540–2961) is classy and expensive—like the Hessischer Hof Hotel in which it's found. It's been the meeting place of the business elite since 1951, and what every other bar in town would like to be. The ladies are more svelte, the gentlemen more charming, the pianist more soothing. The barstools and lounge chairs are of red leather, the bar of mahogany. There is hot food from the hotel kitchen till 3 AM. You must ring the doorbell to get in. Regulars have a key.

The **Luna Bar** (Stiftstr. 6, tel. 069/294–774) is a cocktail-lovers' paradise, with good drinks at reasonable prices by Frankfurt standards. Dress is smart but casual, and there is live music twice a month.

Men without a female companion—or a necktie—can forget about patronizing the elegant **Monza** disco (Grosser Hirschgraben 20, tel. 069/292–518). They should get there early, too, if they want to attend the Friday night "Juice" party or the Saturday night "Love Supreme" with live jazz.

Few people over 25 are trusted at the **Stereo Bar** (Abstgässchen 7, tel. 069/617–116), which has the cheapest drinks in town. You'll find it in a former wine cellar beneath a narrow Sachsenhausen alleyway. The carpeted walls are bright red, there's an aquarium and a tiny dance floor. DJs usually spin the music, though there are occasional live acts.

If you're dressed well enough to get past the doorman, you can join members of the financial community taking their ease at the **Studio Bar** (Katharinenpforte 6, tel. 069/1337–9225). Comfortably grouped sofas and easy chairs make it simple to socialize, and there's a rooftop terrace for summer nights. The selection of drinks at the kidney-shape bar could use some improvement, though.

The **Galerie** discotheque and club (Düsseldorfer Str. 1–7, tel. 069/230–171) doubles as an art museum. Among its special evenings are the monthly "SuperFlirt" parties for singles and, at Easter, a "Bunny Night," with both the chocolate and voluptuous varieties.

DANCE AND NIGHTCLUBS

The Brotfabrik (Bachmannstr. 2–4, tel. 069/9784-5512), a former industrial bakery, is in a desolate part of town, but all is lively inside. Most of the live dance music has a Latin beat— tango on Monday, salsa on Wednesday. But its impressive main hall is the venue for live concerts by visiting jazz groups.

Beneath the heating pipes of a former brewery, **King Kamehameha** (Hanauer Landstr. 192, tel. 069/4059–1194) is designed to suit every type of night owl, whether he or she wishes to drink, relax in a quiet cocktail bar, dance to a house band, or see one of the many live concerts, cabarets, comedy acts, or fashion shows that take place on stage. It's closed Monday.

Trendy **Living XXL** (Kaiserstr. 29, tel. 069/242–9370) is one of the biggest bar-restaurants in Germany and is as hyped as the Eurotower in which it's located, the headquarters of the newly established European Central Bank. On Friday and Saturday it offers a "subdued" disco, geared to the easy-listening preferences of the banking community, but it's not so prudish as to exclude regular gay entertainment. Its spacious, terraced interior has drawn praise for its architecture.

Opium (Am Salzhaus 4, tel. 069/9784–5512), a candlelit disco and club with gilt statues and red walls, presents a strange combination of cultures. On Monday night it has a "Body and Soul" party with an emphasis on soul, yet the cuisine has an Asian note.

There's not much that doesn't take place at the **Tigerpalast** (Heiligkreuzg. 16–20, tel. 069/9200–2250). The best variety shows and circus performances entertain guests, who dine elegantly and get in some dancing in themselves. Shows often sell out, so book tickets as far in advance as possible. It's closed Monday.

JAZZ

The oldest jazz cellar in Germany, **Der Frankfurter Jazzkeller** (Kleine Bockenheimer Str. 18a, tel. 069/288–537) was founded by legendary trumpeter Carlo Bohländer, and has hosted the likes of Louis Armstrong. It offers hot, modern jazz, often free (but the cover charge for some performances is around DM 25/€12.50). It's closed Monday.

Anything can happen at **Dreikönigskeller** (Färberstr. 71, tel. 069/629–273). You might hear 1940s or 1950s jazz, blues, funk, rock-wave, or indie-punk. It's patronized mostly by students, as well as a sprinkling of older, hip people, all smoking as voraciously as the musicians.

Sinkkasten (Brönnerstr. 5–9, tel. 069/280–385), a Frankfurt musical institution, is a class act—a great place for jazz, rock, pop, and African music, often by unknown or hardly-known groups. It's sometimes hard to get in, but worth the effort. There's live music Tuesday–Wednesday and weekends.

LIVE MUSIC

Battschapp (Maybachstr. 24, tel. 069/952–184), with very good acoustics, is the Frankfurt venue for touring international rock acts. It is in an outlying part of the city, near the Eschersheim station on the S6 suburban line.

Music groups from around the world please the thirtysomething fans that make up most of the patronage at **Blues & Beyond** (Berger Str. 159, tel. 069/282–772). Music is live Thursday–Saturday; there are a jam session Monday and a dance night on Wednesday.

Cooky's (Am Salzhaus 4, tel. 069/287–662) is open into the wee hours and is one of the most popular local haunts for rock music; live bands perform on Monday night. You can also dance and have a meal.

WINE CELLARS

Enter the **Bockenheimer Weinkontor** (Schlossstr. 92, tel. 069/702–031) by passing through a courtyard and descending a steep flight of stairs. There's a terrace where wine lovers can sit in summer under a vine-covered shelter.

Popular with crowds before and after performances at the nearby Old Opera, **Vinum** (9 Kleine Hochstr., tel. 069/293–037) is in a vaulted cellar lined with wine kegs. The food, unlike the wine, is overpriced.

Frankfurt's gabled emblem and city hall, the Römer, is hardly big enough for anything but the mayor's office and ceremonial rooms. But it does make room for the **Weinstube im Römer** (Römerberg 19, tel. 069/291–331), one of the few places where you can get wine from Frankfurt's city-owned vineyard on the Lohrberg.

In This Chapter

where to stay

BUSINESSPEOPLE DESCEND ON FRANKFURT year-round, so most hotels in the city are expensive (though many also offer significant reductions on weekends) and are frequently booked up well in advance. Many hotels add as much as a 50% surcharge during trade fairs (Messen), of which there are about 30 a year. If you want to avoid traveling here when trade shows are held, you can check the schedule with the German National Tourist Office. The majority of the larger hotels are close to the main train station, fairgrounds, and business district (Bankenviertel) and are a 20-minute walk from the Old Town. Lower prices and—for some, anyway—more atmosphere are found at smaller hotels and pensions in the suburbs; the efficient public transportation network makes them easy to reach.

CATEGORY	COST*
$$$$	over DM 400/€205
$$$	DM 250/€128–DM 400/€205
$$	DM 150/€77–DM 250/€128
$	under DM 150/€77

*All prices are for two people in a double room, including tax and service.

CITY CENTER

$$$$ ARABELLA SHERATON GRAND. The emphasis here is on the "grand." Everything is large scale, from the palatial public spaces to the vast guest rooms. The center city location means that many rooms have views of backyards and parking lots, but pull

frankfurt lodging

KEY

- *i* Tourist Information
- **S** S-Bahn
- **U** U-Bahn

City Center

Arabella Sheraton Grand, 3

Hessischer Hof, 12

Hilton Frankfurt, 4

Hotel Glockshuber, 19

Hotel Nizza, 15

Le Meridien Parkhotel, 16

Maritim Hotel, 11

Marriott, 10

Pension Aller, 18

Steigenberger Hotel Frankfurter Hof, 14

Terminus, 17

Nordend

Hotel Villa Orange, 2

Outer Frankfurt

Dorint Hotel, 24

Pension Stella, 1

Sheraton Frankfurt, 22

Steigenberger Esprix Hotel, 23

Waldhotel Hensels Felsenkeller, 21

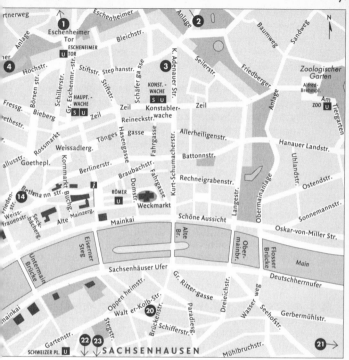

Sachsenhausen	Westend
Maingau, **20**	An der Messe, **7**
	Art Hotel Robert Mayer, **9**
	Hotel Westend, **6**
	Hotel-Pension West, **8**
	Palmenhof, **5**
	Pension Bruns, **13**

the heavy drapes and it's a world of understated luxury. Konrad-Adenauer-Str. 7, 60313, tel. 069/2981–0, fax 069/2981–810, www.arabellasheraton.com. 378 rooms, 11 suites. 2 restaurants, bar, breakfast room, minibar, room service, indoor pool, sauna, health club, meeting rooms, parking (fee). AE, DC, MC, V.

$$$$ HESSISCHER HOF. This is the choice of many businesspeople, not just because it's near the fairgrounds but for the air of class that pervades its handsome and imposing interior (the exterior is nondescript). Many of the public room furnishings are antiques owned by the family of the Princes of Hessen, and Jackie Kennedy was so enthralled by the wallpaper in her room that she had it copied for the White House. Rooms are today done in either a British or Biedermeyer style. The Sèvres Restaurant, so called for the fine display of that porcelain arranged along the walls, features excellent contemporary cuisine. Jimmy's is one of the cult bars in town. Friedrich-Ebert-Anlage 40, D–60325. tel. 069/75400, fax 069/7540–2924, www.hessischer-hof.de. 100 rooms, 17 suites. Restaurant, bar, in-room data ports, breakfast room, minibar, no smoking rooms, room service, meeting rooms, parking (fee). AE, DC, MC, V.

$$$$ HILTON FRANKFURT. This respected chain hotel opened in 1999 with all the perks the business traveler wants, from fax and modem lines to voice mail and video on command. Its Pacific Colors Restaurant has a large terrace overlooking a park. The Vista Bar & Lounge is just below the hotel's airy and transparent atrium. Hochstr. 4, D–60313, tel. 069/133–8000, fax 069/1338–1338, www.hilton.com. 342 rooms. Restaurant, 2 bars, air-conditioning, in-room data ports, in-room safes, minibars, room service, pool, beauty salon, hot tub, massage, sauna, steam room, health club, meeting room, parking (fee). AE, DC, MC, V.

$$$–$$$$ LE MERIDIEN PARKHOTEL. A member of the Forte Group, this reliable hotel has at once the atmosphere of old-time Germany (the Le Parc restaurant is reminiscent of a winter garden) and the services a modern business traveler expects. The old part, the palace, dates from 1905 and is furnished in Old English style. A much more recent wing is modern, functional—and cheaper, if a bit cold in character. It's on a quiet green square just far enough from the main station to avoid the bustle, and most rooms face away from the noise of the street. *Wiesenhuttenpl. 28–38, D–60329, tel. 069/26970, fax 060/269–7884, www.lemeridien.com. 280 rooms, 16 suites. 2 restaurants, bar, breakfast room, Weinstube, in-room data ports, minibar, room service, sauna, gym, parking (fee). AE, DC, MC, V.*

\$\$\$–\$\$\$\$ MARITIM HOTEL. Part of the fairgrounds itself, this brand-new hotel was designed from the ground up with the fair goer in mind. The Messe's new Conference Center shares the building. Rooms have three telephones with answering machines, fax modems, and a safe large enough for a laptop. Its underground garage couldn't be handier to the fair, there is every sort of shop from art and jewelry to antiques and wine, plus Italian, Japanese, and international restaurants. *Theodor-Heuss-Allee 3, D–60486, tel. 069/75780, fax 069/7578–1000, www.maritim-hotels.de. 531 rooms, 24 suites. 3 restaurants, bar, breakfast room, minibar, room service, indoor pool, sauna, shops, meeting rooms, parking (fee). AE, DC, MC, V.*

\$\$\$–\$\$\$\$ MARRIOTT. Europe's tallest hotel is a typical Marriott with a great location across the street from the fairgrounds. It has a business center with computers, secretaries, and all other business needs, plus a pretty good gym with a small spa, massages, and juice bar. The concierge staff is excellent and can make American business travelers feel right at home. The restaurant's food is quite average, but the room service is prompt. The Champions Bar is great for American cocktails, finger food, and TV sports. *Hamburger Allee 2–10, D–60486, tel. 069/79550, fax 069/7955–2432, www.marriotthotels.com. 588 rooms, 24 suites. Restaurant, bar, breakfast room, café, sushi bar, minibar, in-room data* ports, room service, hair salon, sauna, health club, meeting rooms, parking (fee). AE, DC, MC, V.

$$$–$$$$ **STEIGENBERGER HOTEL FRANKFURTER HOF.** The Victorian
★ Frankfurter Hof is one of the city's oldest hotels. Although it fronts on a courtyard, you must enter it through a modest side entrance. The atmosphere throughout is one of old-fashioned, formal elegance, with burnished woods, fresh flowers, and thick-carpeted hush. Kaiser Wilhelm once slept here and world leaders continue to do so. *Am Kaiserpl., D–60311, tel. 069/21502, fax 069/215–900, www.frankfurter-hof.steigenberger.com. 332 rooms, 10 suites. 2 restaurants, breakfast room, in-room data ports, minibars, no-smoking rooms, room service, sauna, concierge, meeting rooms, parking (fee). AE, DC, MC, V.*

$$ **HOTEL NIZZA.** This beautiful Victorian building is furnished with selected antiques, and the proprietor added a modern touch in three bathrooms with her own artistic murals. The name of the hotel reflects the lush Mediterranean flora of its roof garden, where you can have breakfast in good weather with views of rooftops and the skyline. *Elbestr. 10, D–60329, tel. 069/242–5380, fax 069/2425–3830. 24 rooms, 18 with bath. Breakfast room. MC, V.*

$–$$ **HOTEL GLOCKSHUBER.** Near the main train station, this friendly hotel has spacious, bright rooms, but it is on a busy, rather seedy street. Rooms share a shower on each floor. *Mainzer Landstr. 120, D–60327, tel. 069/742–628, fax 069/742–629. 20 rooms with shared showers. Breakfast room. AE, DC, V.*

$–$$ **PENSION ALLER.** Quiet, solid comforts for a modest price and a friendly welcome are right near the train station. The third floor of a sociologist's private home offers cozy, well-lighted rooms in the back of the building. Reserve in advance because it gets a lot of return guests. *Gutleutstr. 94, D–60329, tel. 069/252–596, fax 069/232–330. 10 rooms with shower. No credit cards.*

$ TERMINUS. Directly across the street from the main train station, this modern, sparkling clean hotel has its own underground garage and a restaurant that stays open until 4 AM. It somehow also manages to keep a quiet summer garden despite its location. Though one of the least expensive accommodations in town, the hotel provides each room with a bath, TV, and telephone. *Münchener Str. 59, D–60329, tel. 069/242–320, fax 069/237–411. 107 rooms. Restaurant, breakfast room, parking (fee). AE, DC, MC, V.*

WESTEND

$$$–$$$$ AN DER MESSE. This little place a couple of blocks from the fairgrounds provides a pleasant alternative to the giant hotels of the city. It's stylish, with a pink marble lobby and chicly appointed bedrooms. The staff is courteously efficient. The only drawback is the lack of a restaurant. *Westendstr. 104, D–60325, tel. 069/747–979, fax 069/748–349. 46 rooms, 2 suites. AE, DC, MC, V.*

$$$–$$$$ PALMENHOF. Near the botanical garden, this luxuriously modern
★ hotel occupies a renovated Jugendstil (Art Nouveau) building. The high-ceiling rooms have up-to-date comfort but retain the elegance of the old building. In the basement is a cozy restaurant, L'Artechoc, with a Mediterranean menu. *Bockenheimer Landstr. 89–91, D–60325, tel. 069/753–0060, fax 069/7530–0666. 43 rooms, 37 apartments, 2 suites. Restaurant, parking (fee). AE, DC, MC, V.*

$$–$$$$ HOTEL WESTEND. "Klein aber fein" ("small but nice") is how Germans describe a place like this. Everywhere you turn in this stylish, family-run establishment, you'll trip over French antiques. The hotel itself has no restaurant, but the classy neighborhood has plenty. *Westendstr. 15, D–60325, tel. 069/7898–8180, fax 069/745–396. 20 rooms, 15 with bath or shower. AE, DC, MC, V.*

$$$ ART HOTEL ROBERT MAYER. For creative types who shun the
★ sterile decor of hotel chains, this elegant villa dating from 1905 offers an alternative: 11 rooms, each decorated by a different Frankfurt artist, with furniture designs by the likes of Rietveld and

Frank Lloyd Wright. The room designed by Therese Traube contrasts abstract newspaper collage with a replica Louis XIV armchair. The art tradition is stressed in a special weekend arrangement that includes an individual guided tour of an art museum. It has no restaurant, but a large breakfast buffet is included in the price of the room. *Robert-Mayer-Str. 44, D–60486, tel. 069/970–9100, fax 069/9709–1010, www.art-hotel-robert-mayer.de. 11 rooms, 1 suite. Breakfast room. AE, DC, MC, V.*

$$ HOTEL-PENSION WEST. For home comforts, a handy location (near the university and U-Bahn), and good value, try this family-run pension. It's in an older building and scores high for old-fashioned appeal. The rooms are more than adequate for a night or two. *Gräfstr. 81, D–60486, tel. 069/247–9020, fax 069/707–5309. 15 rooms. AE, DC, MC, V.*

$ PENSION BRUNS. The spacious and airy (but slightly run-down) rooms here have hardwood floors and comfortable beds. The management of this family-run establishment isn't the friendliest, but the pension is near the main train station and the fairgrounds, and the rooms are a deal if you don't mind sharing the bath. Each room does have a sink. Breakfasts are ample and served in your room. *Mendelssohnstr. 42, D–60325, tel. 069/748–896, fax 069/748–846, www.brunsgallus-hotel.de. 9 rooms, one with bath. No credit cards.*

NORDEND

$$–$$$$ HOTEL VILLA ORANGE. Housed in an ornate turn-of-the-20th-century building, the hotel serves business travelers with modem connections in every room, conference facilities, a library, and a lounge with bar. But if the pace of modern life gets too hectic, they can always retreat to rooms with four-poster beds and claw-footed bathtubs. The hotel is handy to the nightspots and restaurants in the new "in" district of Nordend. *Hebelstr. 1, D–60318, tel. 069/405–840, fax 069/4058–4100, www.villa-orange.de. 38 rooms.*

Bar, breakfast room, in-room data ports, no smoking floor, library, meeting rooms, parking (fee). AE, DC, MC, V.

SACHSENHAUSEN

$–$$$ MAINGAU. You'll find this pleasant hotel-restaurant in the middle of the lively Sachsenhausen quarter. Rooms are modest but spotless, comfortable, and equipped with TVs; the room rate includes a substantial breakfast buffet. Chef Werner Döpfner has made the restaurant, Maingau-Stuben, one of Frankfurt's best. (Caution: though the hotel is inexpensive, the restaurant is anything but!) *Schifferstr. 38–40, D–60594, tel. 069/609–140, fax 069/620–790. 100 rooms. Restaurant, minibars, room service, meeting rooms. AE, MC, V.*

OUTER FRANKFURT

$$$–$$$$ DORINT HOTEL. The Frankfurt member of the Dorint chain is a modern, well-appointed hotel with all the comforts and facilities expected from this well-run group, including an indoor pool. The hotel is south of the river in the Niederrad district, but there are good bus and subway connections with the city center and Sachsenhausen. *Hahnstr. 9, D–60528 Frankfurt-Niederrad, tel. 069/663–060, fax 069/6630–6600, www.dorint.de. 191 rooms, 8 suites. 2 restaurants, bar, no-smoking room, indoor pool, sauna, parking (fee). AE, DC, MC, V.*

$$$–$$$$ SHERATON FRANKFURT. This huge hotel is immediately accessible to one of Frankfurt Airport's terminals. It, like the airport, is also adjacent to the Frankfurter Kreuz, the major autobahn intersection, with superhighway connections to all of Europe. Not to worry about noise, the rooms are all soundproofed. In addition to the usual comforts, each room is equipped with an answering machine and a modem. Forty-four of the rooms have ISDN connections that permit a fax machine, printer, and copier. *Hugo-Eckener-Ring 15, Flughafen Terminal 1, D–60594, tel. 069/69770, fax 069/6977–2209, www.sheraton.com. 1,020 rooms, 30 suites. 3 restaurants, 2 bars, in-*

room data ports, minibars, pool, massage, sauna, steam room, gym, concierge, meeting room, parking. AE, DC, MC, V.

$–$$ STEIGENBERGER ESPRIX HOTEL. This new airport hotel, done in cheery primary colors, is the most economical one in the area. It's across the runway from the main terminal buildings and can be reached via the autobahn or a regular shuttle from the airport. Rooms are soundproofed, and the age of flight is the theme design throughout. Decorated with aircraft nostalgia, the Ju 52 bar is named after the celebrated 1930s German transport plane that was the basis of the European air age. *Cargo City Süd, D–60549, tel. 069/697–099, fax 069/6970–9444, www.frankfurt.esprix-hotels.com. 348 rooms, 14 suites. Restaurant, pub, minibars, in-room data ports, sauna, gym, meeting rooms, airport shuttle, parking (fee). AE, DC, MC, V.*

$ PENSION STELLA. This little hostelry is in one of the most pleasant old neighborhoods in town, an area of villas between a park and the studios of Hessischer Rundfunk. Though the desk clerk is gruff and unfriendly, the four rooms, each with bath or shower, are comfortable and the price is right. *Frauensteinstr. 6, D–60322, tel./fax 069/554–026. 4 rooms. Parking (free). No credit cards.*

$ WALDHOTEL HENSELS FELSENKELLER. It's a considerable walk from public transportation, especially if you're carrying luggage, but it's clean, very inexpensive, and in a beautiful location right on the edge of the city forest. Rooms are basic; the less expensive ones have shared showers. *Buchrainstr. 95, D–60599, tel. 069/652–086, fax 069/658–379. 16 rooms, 7 with bath. Restaurant. MC, V.*

Hotel How-Tos

Where you stay does make a difference. Do you prefer a modern high-rise or an intimate B&B? A center-city location or the quiet suburbs? What facilities do you want? Sort through your priorities, then price it all out.

HOW TO GET A DEAL After you've chosen a likely candidate or two, phone them directly and price a room for your travel dates. Then call the hotel's toll-free number and ask the same questions. Also try consolidators and hotel-room discounters. You won't hear the same rates twice. On the spot, make a reservation as soon as you are quoted a price you want to pay.

PROMISES, PROMISES If you have special requests, make them when you reserve. Get written confirmation of any promises.

SETTLE IN Upon arriving, make sure everything works—lights and lamps, TV and radio, sink, tub, shower, and anything else that matters. Report any problems immediately. And don't wait until you need extra pillows or blankets or an ironing board to call housekeeping. Also check out the fire emergency instructions. Know where to find the fire exits, and make sure your companions do, too.

IF YOU NEED TO COMPLAIN Be polite but firm. Explain the problem to the person in charge. Suggest a course of action. If you aren't satisfied, repeat your requests to the manager. Document everything: Take pictures and keep a written record of who you've spoken with, when, and what was said. Contact your travel agent, if he made the reservations.

KNOW THE SCORE When you go out, take your hotel's business cards (one for everyone in your party). If you have extras, you can give them out to new acquaintances who want to call you.

TIP UP FRONT For special services, a tip or partial tip in advance can work wonders.

USE ALL THE HOTEL RESOURCES A concierge can make difficult things easy. But a desk clerk, bellhop, or other hotel employee who's friendly, smart, and ambitious can often steer you straight as well. A gratuity is in order if the advice is helpful.

In This Chapter

side trips

A QUICK TRIP outbound on the local transportation system brings you to Höchst, Neu-Isenburg, and the Taunus hills, which include the picturesque towns of Bad Homberg and Kronberg. Just to the northwest and west of Frankfurt, the Taunus is an area of mixed pine and hardwood forest, medieval castles, and photogenic towns that many Frankfurters regard as their own backyard. This is where bankers and businesspeople unwind on the weekends: hiking through the hills, climbing the Grosser Feldberg, taking the waters at Bad Homburg's healthful mineral springs, or just lazing in elegant stretches of parkland.

Frankfurt is so centrally located in Germany that the list of possible excursions—day trips and longer treks—is nearly endless. Keep in mind that destinations within an hour's drive are Mainz and the Rhineland to the west, Heidelberg and the Neckar Valley to the south, and Würzburg and Franconia to the southeast.

A drive north on the A–5 will take you to Bad Homburg in 30–45 minutes. You can get to Kronberg in about the same amount of time by taking the A–66 (Frankfurt–Wiesbaden) to the Nordwestkreuz interchange and following the signs to Eschborn and Kronberg. Bad Homburg and Kronberg are easily reached by the S-Bahn from Hauptwache, the main train station, and other points in downtown Frankfurt. The S–5 goes to Bad Homburg, the S–4 to Kronberg. There is also a Taunusbahn (from the main station only) that stops in Bad

Homburg and then continues into the far Taunus, including the Römerkastell-Saalburg and Hessenpark.

BAD HOMBURG

The Taunus hills area has many royal associations. Emperor Wilhelm II, the infamous Kaiser of World War I, spent a month each year at Bad Homburg, the area's principal city. And it was the Kaiser's mother, the daughter of Britain's Queen Victoria, who built the magnificent palace, now a luxurious hotel, in the Taunus town of Kronberg. Another frequent visitor to Bad Homburg was Britain's Prince of Wales, later King Edward VII, who made the name Homburg world famous by attaching it to a hat. Until recent decades the Homburg hat was the headgear of preference for diplomats, state dignitaries, and other distinguished gentlemen worldwide. It remains in occasional use and still is manufactured.

Bad Homburg's greatest attraction has always been the **Kurpark** (spa) in the heart of the Old Town, with more than 31 fountains. Romans first used the springs, which were rediscovered and made famous in the 19th century. In the park you'll find not only the popular, highly saline Elisabethenbrunnen spring but also a Siamese temple and a Russian chapel, mementos left by more royal guests—King Chulalongkorn of Siam and Czar Nicholas II. The Kurpark is a good place to begin a walking tour of the town; Bad Homburg's **Tourist Office** (Louisenstr. 5–8, tel. 06172/ 17010) is in the nearby Kurhaus, between Paul-Ehrlich-Weg and Kaiser-Friedrich-Promenade.

Bad Homburg's **Casino,** next to the Kurpark, boasts with some justice that it is the "Mother of Monte Carlo." The original casino in Bad Homburg, one of the world's first, was established in 1841, but closed down in 1866 because Prussian law forbade gambling. The proprietors moved their operation to the French Riviera, and the Bad Homburg casino wasn't reopened until 1949. A bus runs between the casino and Frankfurt's

Hauptbahnhof (south side). It leaves Frankfurt every hour on the hour between 2 PM and 10 PM and then hourly from 10:25 AM to 1:25 AM. Buses back to Frankfurt run every hour on the hour, from 3 PM to the casino's closing. The DM 12/€6 fare will be refunded after the casino's full entry fee has been deducted. *Im Kurpark, tel. 06172/17010.* DM 5/€2.50 for the full gaming area, DM 2/€1.05 for slot machines only. Slot machines 2 PM–1 AM, remainder 3 PM–3 AM.

The most historically noteworthy sight in Bad Homburg is the 17th-century **Schloss,** where the Kaiser stayed when he was in residence. The 172-ft Weisser Turm (White Tower) is all that remains of the medieval castle that once stood here. The Schloss was built between 1680 and 1685 by Friedrich II of Hesse-Homburg, and a few alterations were made in the 19th century. The state apartments are exquisitely furnished, and the Spiegelkabinett (Hall of Mirrors) is especially worthy of a visit. In the surrounding park, look for two venerable trees from Lebanon, both now almost 150 years old. *Schulbergstr., tel. 06172/ 926–2147.* DM 7/€3.60. Mar.–Oct., Tues.–Sun. 10–5; Nov.–Feb., Tues.–Sun. 10–4.

The **Hutmuseum** (Hat Museum), a part of the Museum im Gotischen Haus, is a shrine to headgear. Its collection includes everything from 18th-century tricornered hats to silk toppers, from simple bonnets to the massive, feathered creations of 19th-century milliners. But mainly it's a shrine to the distinguished hat that was developed in Bad Homburg and bears its name. The homburg was made around the turn of the last century for Britain's Prince of Wales, later King Edward VII, a frequent visitor. He liked the shape of the Tyrolean hunting hat but found its green color and decorative feather a bit undignified. So for him Homburg's hatters removed the feather, turned the felt gray, and established an enduring fashion accessory. *Tannenwaldweg 102, tel. 06172/37618. Tues. and Thurs.– Sat. 2–5, Wed. 2–7, Sun. 10–6.*

Just a short, convenient bus ride from Bad Homburg is the highest mountain in the Taunus, the 2,850-ft, eminently hikeable **Grosser Feldberg**.

Only 6½ km (4 mi) from Bad Homburg, and accessible by direct bus service, is the **Römerkastell-Saalburg** (Saalburg Roman Fort). Built in AD 120, the fort could accommodate a cohort (500 men) and was part of the fortifications along the Limes Wall, which ran from the Danube to the Rhine and was meant to protect the Roman Empire from barbarian invasion. On the initiative of Kaiser Wilhelm II, the fort was rebuilt as the Romans left it—with wells, armories, parade grounds, and catapults, as well as shops, houses, baths, and temples. All of these are for viewing only. You can't take a bath or buy a souvenir in the shops, though there is a contemporary restaurant on the grounds. There is also a **museum** with Roman exhibits. The Saalburg is north of Bad Homburg on Route 456 in the direction of Usingen. *Saalburg-Kastell, tel. 06175/93740. DM 5/€2.50. Fort and museum Mar.–Oct., daily 9–6; Nov.–Feb., daily 9–4.*

About a 45-minute walk through the woods along a well-marked path from the Römerkastell-Saalburg is an open-air museum at **Hessenpark**, near Neu Anspach. The museum presents a clear, concrete picture of the world in which 18th- and 19th-century Hessians lived, using 135 acres of rebuilt villages with houses, schools, and farms typical of the time. The park, 15 km (9 mi) outside Bad Homburg in the direction of Usingen, is also accessible from the Frankfurt main station on the Taunusbahn, whose trains run about every half hour until about 9 PM. *Laubweg, Neu-Anspach, tel. 06081/5880. DM 8/€4.10. Mar.–Oct., daily 9–6.*

Where to Stay and Eat

Although most of the well-known spas in Bad Homburg have expensive restaurants, there are still enough affordable places to eat.

$$$$ **STEIGENBERGER BAD HOMBURG.** This member of a prestigious
★ hotel group is a few steps from the casino, downtown, and the
spa park, which many guests find ideal for jogging. The luxurious
rooms are furnished in Art Deco style. Charly's Le Bistro restaurant
serves classical bistro cuisine, but also American and international
dishes. The Sunday morning brunches are popular. *Kaiser-Friedrich-
Promenade 69–75, D–61348, tel. 06172/1810, fax 06172/181–630,
www.bad-homburg.steigenberger.com. 152 rooms, 17 suites. Restaurant,
bar, air-conditioning, in-room data ports, in-room safes, minibars, room
service, sauna, steam room, gym, jogging, laundry service, concierge,
meeting room. AE, DC, MC, V.*

$$$ **MARITIM KURHAUS HOTEL.** Standing in a quiet location on the
edge of the spa park but near the city center, the hotel offers large,
richly furnished rooms with king-size beds and deep armchairs.
Some rooms have balconies. A simple, but uncommon hospitable
perk are the free soft drinks from the minibar. The cozy Bürgerstube,
with local meat dishes and solid German cuisine, is worth a visit
just to see its collection of dolls. For those with early planes to catch,
the hotel serves "early bird breakfasts" from 11 PM to 6:30 AM.
*Ludwigstr. 13, D–61348, tel. 06172/6600, fax 06172/660–100,
www.maritim.de. 148 rooms, 10 suites. Restaurant, bar, 2 cafés, minibars.
AE, DC, MC, V.*

$$$ **SÄNGER'S RESTAURANT.** You'll get a taste of the quintessential
spa experience here: fine dining at high prices. But service is
friendly, and the specialties, calf's head–lobster salad or stuffed
oxtail, may make you forget the bill. *Kaiser-Friedrich-Promenade
85, tel. 06172/928–839. AE, MC. Closed Sun. No lunch Mon. and Sat.*

$$ **ZUM WASSERWEIBCHEN.** Chef Inge Kuper is a local culinary
★ legend. Although prices are high for some items on the menu,
the portions are generous. The clientele sometimes includes
celebrities, and the service is friendly and unpretentious. You
can't go wrong with the potato cakes with salmon mousse, the
brisket of beef, or any of the desserts. *Am Mühlberg 57, tel. 06172/
29878. AE, MC, V. Closed Sat.*

$ KARTOFFELKÜCHE. This simple restaurant serves traditional dishes accompanied by potatoes cooked every way imaginable. The potato and broccoli gratin and the potato pizza are excellent, and for dessert try potato strudel with vanilla sauce. *Audenstr. 4, tel. 06172/21500. AE, DC, MC, V.*

KRONBERG

Another Taunus town, Kronberg, 15 km (9 mi) northwest of Frankfurt, has a magnificent castle-hotel originally built by Queen Victoria, and an open-air zoo. Kronberg's half-timber houses and crooked, winding streets, all on a steep hillside, were so picturesque that an art movement, the Kronberger Malerkolonie, was developed around them. It got started around 1860 when some Frankfurt artists, dismayed by the ugliness of industrialization, retreated to idyllic Kronberg to live and work. The colony grew, once drawing adherents from far off, and lasted until about 1940. The town has a number of the colony's romantic paintings—Kronberg cityscapes and Taunus landscapes—but so far efforts to establish a museum to display them have come to naught.

★ ☺ Established by a very wealthy heir of the man who created the Opel automobile, the large **Opel Zoo** has more than 1,000 native and exotic animals, plus a petting zoo and a playground with more than 100 rides and pieces of equipment. There are also a nature path and a picnic area with grills that can be reserved. Camel and pony rides are offered in the summer. *Königsteiner Str. 35, tel. 06173/79749. DM 12/€6. Apr.–Sept., daily 8:30–6; Oct.–Mar., daily 9–5.*

Where to Stay

$$$$ SCHLOSSHOTEL KRONBERG. It looks like it was built for an empress, and indeed it was. Kaiserin Victoria, daughter of the British queen of the same name and mother of Wilhelm II, the infamous Kaiser of World War I, was empress for only a few

When you pack your MCI Calling Card, it's like packing your loved ones along too.

Your MCI Calling Card is the easy way to stay in touch when you travel. Use it to call to and from over 125 countries. Plus, every time you call, you can earn frequent flier miles. So wherever your travels take you, call home with your MCI Calling Card. It's even easy to get one. Just visit **www.mci.com/worldphone**.

EASY TO CALL WORLDWIDE

1 Just enter the WorldPhone® access number of the country you're calling from.
2 Enter or give the operator your MCI Calling Card number.
3 Enter or give the number you're calling.

Australia ◆	1-800-881-100	Ireland	1-800-55-1001
China	108-12	Italy ◆	172-1022
France ◆	0-800-99-0019	Japan ◆	00539-121▷
Germany	0800-888-8000	South Africa	0800-99-0011
Hong Kong	800-96-1121	Spain	900-99-0014
		United Kingdom	0800-89-0222

◆ Public phones may require deposit of coin or phone card for dial tone. ▷ Regulation does not permit intra-Japan calls.

EARN FREQUENT FLIER MILES

SEE THE WORLD IN FULL COLOR

Fodor's Exploring Guides bring all the great sights vividly to life with hundreds of photographs, fascinating historical background, and colorful anecdotes. Detailed maps and practical information keep you headed in the right direction.

Pair a Fodor's Exploring Guide with your trusted Fodor's Pocket Guide for a complete planning package.

Fodor's EXPLORING GUIDES

At bookstores everywhere.

months, in 1888. This magnificent palace was built for her after she was widowed. It's richly studded with her furnishings and works of art and is surrounded by a park with old trees, a grotto, a rose garden, and an 18-hole golf course. It's one of the few hotels left where you can leave your shoes outside your door for cleaning. Jimmy's Bar, with a pianist, is a local rendezvous. There is free transfer to a nearby fitness center. *Hainstr. 25, D–61476 Kronberg im Taunus, tel. 06173/70101, fax 06173/701267, www.schlosshotel-kronberg.de. 58 rooms and suites. Restaurant bar, no-smoking rooms, room service, concierge, meeting rooms. AE, DC, MC, V.*

HÖCHST

Höchst, a town with a castle and an Altstadt (Old Town) right out of a picture book, has been politically a part of Frankfurt since 1928, though it feels distinctly separate. It can be reached via the S-1 and S-2 suburban trains from Frankfurt's main train station, Hauptwache, and Konstablerwache.

The name *Höchst* is synonymous with chemicals, because of the huge firm that has its headquarters and manufacturing facilities here. Unlike Frankfurt, Höchst was not devastated by wartime bombing, so the castle and the market square, with its half-timber houses, are well preserved. These are well removed from the industrial area, and, indeed, the company Höchst has made major contributions to the Altstadt's fine state of repair. For a week in summer the whole Alstadt is hung with lanterns for the Schlossfest, one of Frankfurt's more popular outdoor festivals.

Höchst was once a porcelain-manufacturing town that rivaled Dresden and Vienna. Production at the **Höchster Porzellan Manufaktur** ceased in the late 18th century but was revived by an enterprising businessman in 1965. Its **outlet** (Berlinerstr. 60, at Kornmarkt, tel. 06109/21700) sells everything from figurines to dinner services, as well as a selection of glassware and silver. *Bolongaro Str. 186, tel. 06109/21700 to arrange a guided tour of the works.*

The **Höchster Schloss,** first built in 1360, houses two **museums,** one about company history and one about Höchst history, the latter with an excellent collection of porcelain. (The castle and a nearby villa were used for decades following the war by the American military broadcaster AFN.) *Museum: Bolongaro Str. at Königsteinerstr., tel. 069/305–7366. Free. Daily 10–4.*

On Bolongaro Strasse, not far from the Höchster Schloss, you can also see a fine exhibit of porcelain at the **Bolongaropalast** (Bolongaro Palace), a magnificent residence facing the river. It was built in the late 18th century by an Italian snuff manufacturer. Its facade—almost the length of a football field—is nothing to sneeze at. *Bolongaro Str. at Königsteinerstr., tel. 069/3106–5520. Free. Daily 10–4.*

Höchst's most interesting attraction is the **Justiniuskirche** (Justinius Church), Frankfurt's oldest building. Dating from the 7th century, the church is part early Romanesque and part 15th-century Gothic. The view from the top of the hill is well worth the walk. *Justiniuspl. at Bolongaro Str.*

Where to Stay

$ HOTEL-SCHIFF PETER SCHLOTT. The hotel ship is moored in the Main River, a 15-minute train or tram ride from the city center. Guest cabins are on the small side, but the river views more than compensate. It's not for you if you're subject to seasickness, but if you like to be rocked to sleep, it's ideal. *Bolongero Str. 25, D–65929, tel. 069/300–4643, fax 069/307–671, hotel-schiff-schlott.de. 19 rooms, 10 with shower. Restaurant. AE, MC, V.*

NEU-ISENBURG

Though an extensive forested area to the south of Frankfurt was leveled in the mid-1930s to make room for the airport, a considerable stretch remains, and Neu-Isenburg is the center of it. At the time of the airport's construction, Germans believed that the future of the air age lay in the lighter-than-air Zeppelin (the 1937 *Hindenburg* disaster lay such notions to rest). **Zeppelinheim,** a once-independent town, now a part of Neu-Isenburg, was constructed to provide hangar space and housing for Zeppelin flight and maintenance crews. Neu-Isenburg can be reached with Streetcar 14 from Frankfurt's Sudbahnhof or with Bus 68 from the airport.

In a forested area just beyond the airport runway, the **Zeppelin Museum** is dedicated to the history of airships in Germany. Exhibits include big, 1:100 models of some of the Zeppelins and a reconstruction of the *Hindenberg*'s promenade deck, with a "view" of Rio de Janeiro. The domed construction gives you the impression you're actually aboard one of the airships. *Kapitän-Lehmann-Str. 2, Neu-Isenburg, tel. 069/694–390. Free. Fri. 1–5, weekends 10–5.*

Where to Stay

$$$–$$$$ GRAVENBRUCH KEMPINSKI. At a parkland site in leafy Neu-
★ Isenburg (a 15-minute drive south of Frankfurt), this sophisticated hotel maintains the atmosphere of the 16th-century manor around which it was built. Some of the luxuriously appointed rooms and suites are arranged as duplex penthouse apartments. Ask for a room overlooking the lake. *An der Bundestr. 459, D–63243 Neu-Isenburg, tel. 06102/5050, fax 06102/505–900, www.kempinski-frankfurt.com. 255 rooms, 28 suites. 2 restaurants, bar, breakfast room, minibars, no smoking rooms, room service, indoor pool, sauna, meeting rooms. AE, DC, MC, V.*

PRACTICAL INFORMATION

Addresses

In this book the words for street (*Strasse*) and alley (*Gasse*) are abbreviated as str. and g. within italicized service information. Saalgasse will appear as Saalg., for example.

Air Travel to and from Frankfurt

BOOKING

When you book **look for nonstop flights** and **remember that "direct" flights stop at least once.** Try to avoid connecting flights, which require a change of plane. For more booking tips and to check prices and make on-line flight reservations, log on to www.fodors.com.

CARRIERS

Major carriers to Frankfurt have nonstop flights from the United States.

➤ MAJOR AIRLINES: **American** (tel. 800/433–7300). **Continental** (tel. 800/525–0280). **Delta** (tel. 800/241–4141. **LTU International Airways** (tel. 800/888–0200). **Lufthansa** (tel. 800/645–3880; 0180/380–3803 in Germany). **Northwest** (tel. 800/225–2525). **United** (tel. 800/241–6522). **US Airways** (tel. 800/428–4322).

➤ FROM THE U.K.: **British Airways** (tel. 0345/222–111). **Lufthansa** (tel. 0345/737–747).

CHECK-IN & BOARDING

Assuming that not everyone with a ticket will show up, airlines routinely overbook planes. When everyone does, airlines ask for volunteers to give up their seats. In return, these volunteers usually get a certificate for a free flight and are rebooked on the next flight out. If there are not enough volunteers, the airline must choose who will be denied boarding. The first to get bumped are passengers who checked in late and those flying on discounted tickets, so **get to the gate and check in as early as possible,** especially during peak periods.

Always **bring a government-issued photo I.D. to the airport;** a passport is best. You may be asked to show it before you are allowed to check in.

CUTTING COSTS

The least expensive airfares to Frankfurt must usually be purchased in advance and are non-refundable. It's smart to **call a number of airlines, and when you are quoted a good price, book it on the spot**—the same fare may not be available the next day. Always **check different routings** and look into using different airports. Travel agents, especially low-fare specialists (☞ Discounts & Deals), are helpful.

Consolidators are another good source. They buy tickets for scheduled international flights at reduced rates from the airlines, then sell them at prices that beat the best fare available directly from the airlines, usually without restrictions. Sometimes you can even get your money back if you need to return the ticket. Carefully read the fine print detailing penalties for changes and cancellations, and **confirm your consolidator reservation with the airline.**

➤ CONSOLIDATORS: **Cheap Tickets** (tel. 800/377–1000). **Discount Airline Ticket Service** (tel. 800/576–1600). **Unitravel** (tel. 800/325–2222). **Up & Away Travel** (tel. 212/889–2345). **World Travel Network** (tel. 800/409–6753).

ENJOYING THE FLIGHT

For more legroom, **request an emergency-aisle seat.** Don't sit in the row in front of the emergency aisle or in front of a bulkhead, where seats may not recline. If you have dietary concerns, **ask for special meals when booking.** These can be vegetarian, low-cholesterol, or kosher, for example. On long flights, try to maintain a normal routine, to help fight jet lag. At night, **get some sleep.** By day, **eat light meals, drink water** (not alcohol), and **move around the cabin** to stretch your legs. For additional jet-lag tips consult *Fodor's FYI: Travel Fit & Healthy* (available at bookstores everywhere).

FLYING TIMES

Flying time to Frankfurt is 7½ hours from New York, 10 hours from Chicago, and 12 hours from Los Angeles.

HOW TO COMPLAIN

If your baggage goes astray or your flight goes awry, complain right away. Most carriers require that you **file a claim immediately.**

➤ AIRLINE COMPLAINTS: U.S. Department of Transportation **Aviation Consumer Protection Division** (C-75, Room 4107, Washington, DC 20590, tel. 202/366–2220, www.dot.gov/airconsumer). **Federal Aviation Administration Consumer Hotline** (tel. 800/322–7873).

Airports & Transfers

Frankfurt Airport is the biggest on the Continent, second in Europe only to London's Heathrow. There are direct flights to Frankfurt from many U.S. cities and from all major European cities. An elevated "Sky Line" connects the airport's two terminals, and the transfer takes about two minutes.

Baggage storage is available at arrivals in Hall B of Terminal 1 (24 hours) and Hall D of Terminal 2 (6 AM–11 PM). An unusual facility are the showers in Terminal 1, next to the waiting lounge in Hall B, and in the Transit area B. The U.S. $6 fee includes towel and soap.

➤ AIRPORT INFORMATION: **Flughafen Frankfurt Main** (tel. 069/6903–0511).

AIRPORT TRANSFERS

The airport is 10 km (6 mi) southwest of the downtown area by the A–5 Autobahn, and getting into Frankfurt is easy. The S-Bahn 8 (suburban train) runs from the airport to downtown.

Most travelers get off at the Hauptbahnhof (main train station) or at Hauptwache, in the heart of Frankfurt. Trains run at least every 15 minutes, and the trip takes about 15 minutes. The one-way fare is DM 6.10/€3.05. A taxi from the airport into the city center normally takes around 20 minutes; allow double the travel time during rush hours. The fare is approximately DM 45/€23. If driving a rental car from the airport, take the main road out of the airport and follow the signs reading STADTMITTE (downtown).

Conveniently connected to Terminal 1 is the AIRail Terminal for long-distance, high-speed InterCity (IC) and InterCity Express (ICE) trains. A shuttle bus from Terminal 2 runs to this rail station every 10 to 15 minutes. Beneath Terminal 1 is the regional train station for local and regional trains.

DUTY-FREE SHOPPING

You can purchase duty-free goods when traveling between any EU country, such as Germany, and a non-EU country. Duty-free (also called tax-free) shops at German airports are operated by the firm of Gebrüder Heinemann. The big sellers, as at most duty-free shops, are perfumes and cosmetics, liquor, and tobacco products.

Bike Travel

There are bike paths beside the arterial streets, field paths exclusively for cyclers and pedestrians, and "traffic calmed" streets where bikes and pedestrians have the right of way. Bikes may also be taken aboard trains and buses at no extra charge, though it's best to avoid doing this during rush hour.

Reserve rental bikes in advance for weekends and holidays. Theo Intra's shop has a large selection of bikes, from tandems to racing models. It's located on the city's northern edge, convenient to the inviting trails of the Taunus hills. Take the U-6 or U-7 to Bockenheimer Warte, then Bus 50 to Carl-

Sonnenschein-Strasse. Bicycles also can be rented at the Hauptbahnhof through Deutsche Bahn for DM 15/€7.70 a day.

➤ BIKE RENTALS: **Deutsche Bahn** (German Railway, tel. 069/2653–4834). **Theo Intra's shop** (Westerbachstr. 273, tel. 069/342–780).

Bus Travel to and from Frankfurt

More than 200 European cities—including most major German cities—have bus links with Frankfurt. Buses arrive and depart from the south side of the Hauptbahnhof.

➤ BUS INFORMATION: **Deutsche Touring** (Am Römerhof 17, tel. 069/790–350. www.touring-germany.com).

Business Hours

BANKS & OFFICES

Banks are generally open weekdays from 8:30 or 9 to 3 or 4 (5 or 6 on Thursday), sometimes with a lunch break of about an hour at smaller branches. Banks at airports and main train stations open as early as 6:30 AM and close as late as 10:30 PM.

GAS STATIONS

Along the autobahn and major highways, gas stations and their small convenience shops are often open late, if not around the clock.

MUSEUMS & SIGHTS

Most museums are open from Tuesday to Sunday 10–5. Some close for an hour or more at lunch. Many stay open until 8 or 9 on Wednesday or Thursday.

SHOPS

Stores are permitted to operate weekdays from 6 AM to 8 PM and Saturday from 6 AM to 4 PM. They must remain closed on Sunday, and the 4 PM closing on Saturday makes for crowded shopping conditions that day. The airport doubles as a mall, whose stores are allowed to ignore the otherwise strict closing hours.

Cameras & Photography

The *Kodak Guide to Shooting Great Travel Pictures* (available at bookstores everywhere) is loaded with tips.

➤ Photo Help: **Kodak Information Center** (tel. 800/242–2424).

EQUIPMENT PRECAUTIONS

Don't pack film and equipment in checked luggage, where it is much more susceptible to damage. X-ray machines used to view checked luggage are becoming much more powerful and therefore are much more likely to ruin your film. Always **keep film and tape out of the sun.** Carry an extra supply of batteries, and **be prepared to turn on your camera or camcorder** to prove to security personnel that the device is real. Always **ask for hand inspection of film,** which becomes clouded after repeated exposure to airport X-ray machines, and **keep videotapes away from metal detectors.**

VIDEOS

The German standard for video is VHS–PAL, which is not compatible with the U.S. VHS–NTSC standard.

Car Rental

Rates with the major car-rental companies begin at about $45 per day and $220 per week, including value added tax, for an economy car with a manual transmission and unlimited mileage. Volkswagen, Opel, and Mercedes are some standard brands of rentals; most rentals are manual, so if you want an automatic, be sure to **request one in advance.** If you're traveling with children, don't forget to **arrange for a car seat** when you reserve.

➤ Major Agencies: **Alamo** (tel. 800/522–9696; 020/8759–6200 in the U.K.). **Avis** (tel. 800/331–1084; 800/879–2847 in Canada; 02/9353–9000 in Australia; 09/525–1982 in New Zealand; 0870/606–0100 in the U.K.). **Budget** (tel. 800/527–0700; 0870/607–5000 in the U.K., through affiliate Europcar). **Dollar** (tel. 800/800–6000; 0124/

622–0111 in the U.K., through affiliate Sixt Kenning; 02/9223–1444 in Australia). **Hertz** (tel. 800/654–3001; 800/263–0600 in Canada; 020/8897–2072 in the U.K.; 02/9669–2444 in Australia; 09/256–8690 in New Zealand). **National Car Rental** (tel. 800/227–7368; 020/8680–4800 in the U.K., where it is known as National Europe).

CUTTING COSTS

To get the best deal, **book through a travel agent who will shop around.** You will get a much better rate by booking in advance from your home country, rather than renting once you arrive in Frankfurt.

Do **look into wholesalers,** companies that do not own fleets but rent in bulk from those that do and often offer better rates than traditional car-rental operations. Payment must be made before you leave home.

➤ LOCAL AGENCIES: **Avis** (Schmidtstr. 39, tel. 069/730–111). **Europcar** (Kennedyallee 280, tel. 069/6772–0291). **Hertz** (Hanauer Landstr. 117, tel. 069/449–090).

➤ WHOLESALERS: **Auto Europe** (tel. 207/842–2000 or 800/223–5555, fax 800/235–6321, www.autoeurope.com). **Europe by Car** (tel. 212/581–3040 or 800/223–1516, fax 212/246–1458, www.europebycar.com). **DER Travel Services** (9501 W. Devon Ave., Rosemont, IL 60018, tel. 800/782–2424, fax 800/282–7474 for information; 800/860–9944 for brochures, www.dertravel.com). **Kemwel Holiday Autos** (tel. 800/678–0678, fax 914/825–3160, www.kemwel.com).

INSURANCE

When driving a rented car, you are generally responsible for any damage to or loss of the vehicle. Before you rent, see what coverage your personal auto-insurance policy and credit cards provide.

Before you buy collision coverage, check your existing policies—you may already be covered. However, collision policies that car-rental companies sell for European rentals usually do not include stolen-vehicle coverage.

REQUIREMENTS & RESTRICTIONS

In Germany your own driver's license is acceptable, but an International Driver's Permit is a good idea; it's available from the American or Canadian automobile association and, in the United Kingdom, from the Automobile Association or Royal Automobile Club. These international permits are universally recognized, and having one in your wallet may save you a problem with the local authorities. In Germany you must usually be 21 to rent a car.

SURCHARGES

Before you pick up a car in one city and leave it in another, **ask about drop-off charges or one-way service fees,** which can be substantial. Note, too, that some rental agencies charge extra if you return the car before the time specified in your contract. To avoid a hefty refueling fee, **fill the tank just before you turn in the car,** but be aware that gas stations near the rental outlet may overcharge.

Car Travel

Bundesstrassen are two-lane highways, abbreviated "B," as in B–38. Autobahns are high-speed thruways abbreviated with "A," as in A–5.

Of the major autobahns that meet in Frankfurt, the most important are the A–3, running south from Köln and then west on to Würzburg, and the A–5, running south from Giessen and then on toward Mannheim and Heidelberg. A complex series of beltways surrounds the city. If you're driving to Frankfurt on the A–5 from either north or south, exit at Nordwestkreuz and follow A–66 to the Nordend district, just north of downtown. Driving south on the A–3, exit onto A–66 and follow the signs to Frankfurt-Höchst and then the Nordwestkreuz interchange. Driving west on the A–3, exit at Offenbacher Kreuz onto A–661 and follow the signs for FRANKFURT-STADTMITTE.

98

EMERGENCY SERVICES

AvD (Automobilclub von Deutschland) operates tow trucks on all autobahns; it also has emergency telephones every 2 km (1 mi). On minor roads **go to the nearest call box and dial 01802/ 222–222** (if you have a mobile phone, just dial 222–222). Ask, in English, for road-service assistance.

➤ **CONTACTS: AvD** (Lyonerstr. 16, D–60528 Frankfurt, tel. 069/ 66060, fax 069/6606–260).

PARKING

There are many reasonably priced parking garages around the downtown area, and a well developed "park and ride" system along the suburban train lines. The transit map shows nearly a hundred outlying stations with a "P" symbol beside them, meaning there is convenient parking there. Within the city, tow trucks cruise the streets in search of illegal parkers. Parking-meter spaces are free at night. In German garages you must **pay immediately on returning to retrieve your car,** not when driving out. Put the ticket you got on arrival into the machine and pay the amount displayed. Retrieve the ticket, go to your car, and upon exiting, insert the ticket in a slot to get the barrier raised.

ROAD MAPS

The best-known road maps of Germany are put out by the automobile club ADAC, by Shell, and by the Falk Verlag. They're available at gas stations and bookstores.

RULES OF THE ROAD

In Germany you **drive on the right,** and road signs give distances in kilometers. There is no speed limit on autobahns, although drivers are advised to keep below 130 kph (80 mph). Speed limits on country roads vary from 80 to 100 kph (50 to 60 mph). Alcohol limits on drivers are equivalent to two small beers or a quarter of a liter of wine (blood-alcohol level .05%). Note that **seat belts must be worn at all times by front- and backseat passengers.** Passing is permitted on the left side only.

Headlights, not parking lights, are required during inclement weather.

TRAFFIC

Driving in Frankfurt can be a headache. Back-ups because of rush-hour traffic, accidents, or construction (or all three) mean that it will take 15 minutes more than anticipated to get anywhere. Speeders are often caught with hidden cameras.

Children in Frankfurt

BABY-SITTING

For recommended local sitters, **check with your hotel desk.** Updated lists of well-screened baby-sitters are also available from most local tourist offices. Rates are usually between DM 15/€8 and DM 25/€13 per hour. Many large department stores in Germany provide baby-sitting facilities or areas where children can play while their parents shop.

LODGING

Many hotels in Germany allow children under three to stay in their parents' room at no extra charge. Older children may be charged half price or even be considered extra adults; be sure to **find out if the cutoff age applies.**

SIGHTS & ATTRACTIONS

Places that are especially appealing to children are indicated in this guide by a rubber-duckie icon (🐤) in the margin.

Computers on the Road

If you use a major Internet provider, getting online in Frankfurt should be easy. Contact your Internet provider to get the local access number for Frankfurt and to find out the surcharge you will be charged. Larger hotels now have Internet centers from which, for a fee, you can access a Web site or send e-mail. There are also plenty of cybercafés at which you can go online, either with their equipment or your own laptop. You may, however, need to buy an appropriate adapter for your laptop's phone jack. If you're traveling with a laptop, carry a spare battery and adapter. Never plug your computer into any socket without asking about surge protection. IBM sells a pen-size modem tester that plugs into a telephone jack to check whether the line is safe to use.

➤ ACCESS NUMBERS IN FRANKFURT: **AOL** (01914; for cell access: 0171–41914 or 0172–22144). **Compuserve** (01088–0191919; for cell access: 0172–22188).

Concierges

Concierges, found in many hotels, can help you with theater tickets and dinner reservations: a good one with connections may be able to get you seats for a hot show or prime-time dinner reservations at the restaurant of the moment. You can also turn to your hotel's concierge for help with travel arrangements, sightseeing plans, services ranging from aromatherapy to zipper repair, and emergencies. Always, **always tip** a concierge who has been of assistance.

Consulates

➤ AUSTRALIA: Grüneburgweg 58–62, D–60322, tel. 069/905–580.

➤ UNITED KINGDOM: Bockenheimer Landstr. 42, D–60323, tel. 069/170–0020.

➤ UNITED STATES: Siesmayerstr. 21, D–60323, tel. 069/75350.

Consumer Protection

Whenever shopping or buying travel services in Frankfurt, **pay with a major credit card,** if possible, so you can cancel payment or get reimbursed if there's a problem. If you're doing business with a particular company for the first time, **contact your local Better Business Bureau and the attorney general's offices** in your state and (for U.S. businesses) the company's home state as well. Have any complaints been filed? Finally, if you're buying a package or tour, always **consider travel insurance** that includes default coverage (☞ Insurance).

➤ **BBBs: Council of Better Business Bureaus** (4200 Wilson Blvd., Suite 800, Arlington, VA 22203, tel. 703/276–0100, fax 703/525–8277, www.bbb.org).

Customs & Duties

When shopping, **keep receipts** for all purchases. Upon reentering the country, **be ready to show customs officials what you've bought.** If you feel a duty is incorrect or object to the way your clearance was handled, note the inspector's badge number and ask to see a supervisor. If the problem isn't resolved, write to the appropriate authorities, beginning with the port director at your point of entry.

IN GERMANY

Since a single, unrestricted market took effect within the European Union (EU) early in 1993, there have no longer been restrictions for persons traveling among the 15 EU countries. However, there are restrictions on what can be brought in without declaration. For example, if you have more than 800 cigarettes, 90 liters of wine, or 10 liters of alcohol, it is considered a commercial shipment and is taxed and otherwise treated as such.

For anyone entering Germany from outside the EU, the following limitations apply: (1) 200 cigarettes or 100 cigarillos or 50 cigars or 250 grams of tobacco; (2) 2 liters of still table wine; (3) 1 liter of spirits over 22% volume or 2 liters of spirits under 22% volume (fortified and sparkling wines) or 2 more liters of table wine; (4) 50 grams of perfume and 250 milliliters of toilet water; (5) 500 grams of roasted coffee or 200 grams of instant coffee; (6) other goods to the value of DM 350/€175.

Tobacco and alcohol allowances are for visitors age 17 and over. Other items intended for personal use can be imported and exported freely. If you try to bring in cash, checks, securities, precious metals, or jewelry with a value of more than DM 30,000/€15,385, you must tell the customs people where you got it and what you intend to do with it. This is a new measure for fighting money laundering.

➤ **INFORMATION: Frankfurt Customs Office** (tel. 069/690–26081).

IN AUSTRALIA

Australian residents who are 18 or older may bring home $A400 worth of souvenirs and gifts (including jewelry), 250 cigarettes or 250 grams of tobacco, and 1,125 ml of alcohol (including wine, beer, and spirits). Residents under 18 may bring back $A200 worth of goods. Prohibited items include meat products. Seeds, plants, and fruits need to be declared upon arrival.

➤ **INFORMATION: Australian Customs Service** (Regional Director, Box 8, Sydney, NSW 2001, Australia, tel. 02/9213–2000, fax 02/9213–4000, www.customs.gov.au).

IN CANADA

Canadian residents who have been out of Canada for at least seven days may bring home C$500 worth of goods duty-free. If you've been away fewer than seven days but more than 48 hours, the duty-free allowance drops to C$200; if your trip lasts 24–48 hours, the allowance is C$50. You may not pool allowances with family members. Goods claimed under the C$500 exemption may follow you by mail; those claimed under the lesser exemptions must accompany you. Alcohol and tobacco products may be included in the seven-day and 48-hour exemptions but not in the 24-hour exemption. If you meet the age requirements of the province or territory through which you reenter Canada, you may bring in, duty-free, 1.14 liters (40 imperial ounces) of wine or liquor or 24 12-ounce cans or bottles of beer or ale. If you are 16 or older you may bring in, duty-free, 200 cigarettes and 50 cigars. Check ahead of time with Revenue Canada or the Department of Agriculture for policies regarding meat products, seeds, plants, and fruits.

You may send an unlimited number of gifts worth up to C$60 each duty-free to Canada. Label the package UNSOLICITED GIFT—VALUE UNDER $60. Alcohol and tobacco are excluded.

➤ **INFORMATION: Revenue Canada** (2265 St. Laurent Blvd. S, Ottawa, Ontario K1G 4K3, Canada, tel. 613/993–0534; 800/461–9999 in Canada, fax 613/991–4126, www.ccra-adrc.gc.ca).

IN NEW ZEALAND

Homeward-bound residents 17 or older may bring back $700 worth of souvenirs and gifts. Your duty-free allowance also includes 4.5 liters of wine or beer; one 1,125-ml bottle of spirits; and either 200 cigarettes, 250 grams of tobacco, 50 cigars, or a combination of the three up to 250 grams. Prohibited items include meat products, seeds, plants, and fruits.

➤ **INFORMATION: New Zealand Customs** (Custom House, 50 Anzac Ave., Box 29, Auckland, New Zealand, tel. 09/300–5399, fax 09/359–6730, www.customs.govt.nz).

IN THE U.K.

If you are a U.K. resident and your journey was wholly within the European Union (EU), you won't have to pass through customs when you return to the United Kingdom. If you plan to bring back large quantities of alcohol or tobacco, check EU limits beforehand.

➤ **INFORMATION: HM Customs and Excise** (Dorset House, Stamford St., Bromley, Kent BR1 1XX, U.K., tel. 020/7202–4227, www.hmce.gov.uk).

IN THE U.S.

U.S. residents who have been out of the country for at least 48 hours (and who have not used the $400 allowance or any part of it in the past 30 days) may bring home $400 worth of foreign goods duty-free.

U.S. residents 21 and older may bring back 1 liter of alcohol duty-free. In addition, regardless of your age, you are allowed 200 cigarettes and 100 non-Cuban cigars. Antiques, which the U.S. Customs Service defines as objects more than 100 years old, enter duty-free, as do original works of art done entirely by hand, including paintings, drawings, and sculptures.

You may also mail or ship packages home duty-free: up to $200 worth of goods for personal use, with a limit of one parcel per addressee per day (except alcohol or tobacco products or perfume worth more than $5); label the package PERSONAL USE and attach a list of its contents and their retail value. Do not label the package UNSOLICITED GIFT or your duty-free exemption will drop to $100. Mailed items do not affect your duty-free allowance on your return.

➤ INFORMATION: **U.S. Customs Service** (1300 Pennsylvania Ave. NW, Washington, DC 20229, www.customs.gov; inquiries tel. 202/354–1000; complaints c/o 1300 Pennsylvania Ave. NW, Room 5.4D, Washington, DC 20229; registration of equipment c/o Resource Management, tel. 202/927–0540).

Dining

Lunch rather than dinner is the traditional main meal in Germany. The *Tageskarte*, or suggested menu, is usually less than DM 20/10 for soup, a main course, and a simple dessert (though the latter is not always offered). It's perfectly acceptable to order just a pot of coffee outside busy lunch periods. More expensive restaurants may offer a *table d'hôte* (suggested or special) daily menu, which is considerably cheaper than paying à la carte. A *Bierstube* (pub) or *Weinstube* (wine cellar) may also serve light snacks or meals.

Frankfurt's regional specialties are discussed in ☞ Eating Out. The restaurants we list are the cream of the crop in each price category.

BUDGET EATING TIPS

There are plenty of ways to eat cheaply while in Frankfurt. Cafeteria-style restaurants in department stores serve wholesome, appetizing, and inexpensive lunches. Galerie Kaufhof and Hertie are names to note. Frankfurt also has a vast selection of moderately priced Turkish, Italian, Greek, Chinese, and Balkan restaurants.

To turn lunch into a picnic, **buy some wine or beer and some cold cuts and rolls** from a supermarket or delicatessen, or a warm snack from a *Metzgerei* (butcher shop). It's acceptable to bring fixings to a beer garden and order a beer there.

Imbiss (snack) stands can be found in almost every busy shopping street, in parking lots, train stations, and near markets. They serve *Würste* (sausages), grilled, roasted, or boiled, and rolls filled with cheese, cold meat, or fish. Prices range from DM 2/€1 to DM 5/€2.50 per portion.

MEALTIMES

Unless otherwise noted, the restaurants listed in this guide are open daily for lunch and dinner.

PAYING

Credit cards are generally accepted only in moderate to expensive restaurants, smaller ones of which may still take only cash. If you plan to pay with credit, always **check the stickers on the door** for credit-card symbols (or ask a waiter) before ordering.

RATINGS

The restaurants in our listings are divided by price (representing the cost of a main course at dinner) into four categories: $$$$, $$$, $$, and $. *See* Eating Out for specific prices. Nearly all restaurants display their menus, with prices, outside; all prices shown will include tax and service charge. Prices for wine also include tax and service charge.

RESERVATIONS & DRESS

Reservations are always a good idea: we mention them only when they're essential or not accepted. Book as far ahead as you can, and reconfirm as soon as you arrive. We mention dress only when men are required to wear a jacket or a jacket and tie.

Disabilities & Accessibility

Nearly all of the Frankfurt museums are disability-friendly, with ramps and elevators, and the Club Behinderter und ihrer

Freunde in Frankfurt und Umgebung (CeBeeF) has a list of disability-friendly hotels. It also has English-speaking personnel who will be happy to see to the needs of any visitor who gives it a call, but its literature and Web site are exclusively in German.

▶ LOCAL RESOURCES: **Bahnhofs-Mission** (tel. 069/234–468). **Club Behinderter und ihrer Freunde in Frankfurt und Umgebung (CeBeeF)** (Insterburgerstr. 12, tel. 069/9798–7721, www.cebeef.com). **Deutsche Bahn hot line** (tel. 01805/996–633).

LODGING

All the major hotel chains (Hilton, Sheraton, Marriott, Holiday Inn, Steigenberger, and Kempinski) have special facilities for guests with disabilities. Some leading privately owned hotels also cater to travelers with disabilities; see ☞ Club Behinderter und ihrer Freunde in Frankfurt und Umgebung (CeBeeF) for these hotels and additional information.

RESERVATIONS

When discussing accessibility with an operator or reservations agent, **ask hard questions.** Are there any stairs, inside or out? Are there grab bars next to the toilet *and* in the shower/tub? How wide is the doorway to the room? To the bathroom? For the most extensive facilities meeting the latest legal specifications, **opt for newer accommodations.**

TRANSPORTATION

An organization called the Bahnhofs-Mission (Railway Station Mission) has an office at the main train station that serves travelers with disabilities. Its staff may, for example, help wheelchair users on and off trains (the station has a device for this purpose), help blind people change trains or get a taxi, and assist in purchasing tickets and making reservations. The Deutsche Bahn issues a booklet, with an English section, detailing its services. Reservations for wheelchair users are free of charge, and all InterCity Express (ICE) and InterRegio trains and most EuroCity and InterCity trains have special areas and toilets for wheelchair users. The Deutsche Bahn's 24-hour hot line can help address special needs, but its best to **call three working days before your trip.**

➤ COMPLAINTS: **Aviation Consumer Protection Division** (☞ Air Travel) for airline-related problems. **Civil Rights Office** (U.S. Department of Transportation, Departmental Office of Civil Rights, S-30, 400 7th St. SW, Room 10215, Washington, DC 20590, tel. 202/366–4648, fax 202/366–9371, www.dot.gov/ost/docr/index.htm) for problems with surface transportation. **Disability Rights Section** (U.S. Department of Justice, Civil Rights Division, Box 66738, Washington, DC 20035-6738, tel. 202/514–0301 or 800/514–0301; 202/514–0383 TTY; 800/514–0383 TTY, fax 202/307–1198, www.usdoj.gov/crt/ada/adahom1.htm) for general complaints.

➤ LOCAL TRANSPORTATION RESOURCES: **Bahnhofs-Mission** (tel. 069/234–468). **Deutsche Bahn hot line** (tel. 01805/996–633).

TRAVEL AGENCIES

In the United States, the Americans with Disabilities Act requires that travel firms serve the needs of all travelers. Some agencies specialize in working with people with disabilities.

➤ TRAVELERS WITH MOBILITY PROBLEMS: **Access Adventures** (206 Chestnut Ridge Rd., Scottsville, NY 14624, tel. 716/889–9096), run by a former physical-rehabilitation counselor. **CareVacations** (5-5110 50th Ave., Leduc, Alberta T9E 6V4, Canada, tel. 780/986–6404 or 877/478–7827, fax 780/986–8332, www.carevacations.com), for group tours and cruise vacations. **Flying Wheels Travel** (143 W. Bridge St., Box 382, Owatonna, MN 55060, tel. 507/451–5005 or 800/535–6790, fax 507/451–1685, www.flyingwheelstravel.com).

Discounts & Deals

Be a smart shopper and **compare all your options** before making decisions. A plane ticket bought with a promotional coupon from travel clubs, coupon books, and direct-mail offers or on the Internet may not be cheaper than the least expensive fare from a discount ticket agency. And always keep in mind that what you get is just as important as what you save.

DISCOUNT RESERVATIONS

To save money, **look into discount reservations services** with toll-free numbers, which use their buying power to get a better price on hotels, airline tickets, even car rentals. When booking a room, always **call the hotel's local toll-free number** (if one is available) rather than the central reservations number—you'll often get a better price. Always ask about special packages or corporate rates.

When shopping for the best deal on hotels and car rentals, **look for guaranteed exchange rates,** which protect you against a falling dollar. With your rate locked in, you won't pay more, even if the price goes up in the local currency.

➤ AIRLINE TICKETS: tel. 800/FLY–ASAP.

➤ HOTEL ROOMS: **Players Express Vacations** (tel. 800/458–6161, www.playersexpress.com). **Travel Interlink** (tel. 800/888–5898, www.travelinterlink.com). **Turbotrip.com** (tel. 800/473–7829, www.turbotrip.com).

PACKAGE DEALS

Don't confuse packages and guided tours. When you buy a package, you travel on your own, just as though you had planned the trip yourself. Fly/drive packages, which combine airfare and car rental, are often a good deal. In cities, ask the local visitors' bureau about hotel packages that include tickets to major museum exhibits or other special events.

Electricity

To use electrical devices purchased in the U.S. or Canada, **bring a converter and adapter.** The electrical current in Germany is 220 volts, 50 cycles alternating current (AC); wall outlets take Continental-type plugs, with two round prongs.

If your appliances are dual-voltage, you'll need only an adapter. Don't use 110-volt outlets marked FOR SHAVERS ONLY for high-wattage appliances such as blow-dryers. Most laptops operate equally well on 110 and 220 volts and so require only an adapter.

Emergencies

➤ **AMBULANCE AND FIRE SERVICES:** tel. 112.

➤ **DENTISTS:** tel. 069/660–7271.

➤ **DOCTORS:** tel. 069/19292.

➤ **POLICE:** tel. 110.

➤ **24-HOUR PHARMACIES AND PET DOCTORS:** tel. 069/011500.

English-Language Media

➤ **BOOKSTORES: British Bookshop** (Börsenstr. 17, tel. 069/280–492).

NEWSPAPERS & MAGAZINES

Frankfurt does not have an English-language magazine. A local newspaper, the *Frankfurter Allgemeine Zeitung,* has an English-language edition, distributed daily as a supplement to the *International Herald Tribune,* but it carries no local news. The IHT is widely available at newsstands, as are such Americans publications as *USA Today, Time,* and *Newsweek,* and such British publications as the *Daily Mail, Daily Telegraph,* and *Times.* The international newsstands at the main train station, the airport, and the Haupwache subway station carry hundreds of English-language newspapers, magazines, and paperbacks.

RADIO & TELEVISION

Though most of the U.S. military has now moved out of Frankfurt, the American Forces Network, the celebrated soldiers' broadcaster, continues to operate in studios right next to the Hessischer Rundfunk, presenting American news, sports, and music. Its radio signal is easy to get in the Frankfurt area. Its AM broadcast (primarily talk) is at 873; the FM signal (primarily music) is at 98.7.

Etiquette & Behavior

Germans are more formal in addressing each other than Americans are. Always address acquaintances as Herr (Mr.) or Frau (Mrs.) plus their last name; do not call them by their first name unless invited to do so. The German language has both a formal and an informal pronoun for "you": formal is *Sie*, informal is *du*. Even if adults are on a first-name basis, they may still keep to the *Sie* form between them. A handshake is expected upon meeting someone for the first time and is often customary when simply greeting acquaintances.

Gay & Lesbian Travel

▶ GAY- & LESBIAN-FRIENDLY TRAVEL AGENCIES: **Different Roads Travel** (8383 Wilshire Blvd., Suite 902, Beverly Hills, CA 90211, tel. 323/651–5557 or 800/429–8747, fax 323/651–3678). **Kennedy Travel** (314 Jericho Turnpike, Floral Park, NY 11001, tel. 516/352–4888 or 800/237–7433, fax 516/354–8849, www.kennedytravel.com). **Now Voyager** (4406 18th St., San Francisco, CA 94114, tel. 415/626–1169 or 800/255–6951, fax 415/626–8626, www.nowvoyager.com). **Skylink Travel and Tour** (1006 Mendocino Ave., Santa Rosa, CA 95401, tel. 707/546–9888 or 800/225–5759, fax 707/546–9891, www.skylinktravel.com), serving lesbian travelers.

Holidays

The following national holidays are observed in Germany: January 1; Good Friday; Easter Monday; May 1 (Workers' Day); Ascension and Pentecost Monday; October 3 (German Unity Day); December 24–26 (Christmas).

Insurance

The most useful travel-insurance plan is a comprehensive policy that includes coverage for trip cancellation and interruption, default, trip delay, and medical expenses (with a waiver for pre-existing conditions).

Without insurance you will lose all or most of your money if you cancel your trip, regardless of the reason. Default insurance covers you if your tour operator, airline, or cruise line goes out of business. Trip-delay covers expenses that arise because of bad weather or mechanical delays. Study the fine print when comparing policies.

If you're traveling internationally, a key component of travel insurance is coverage for medical bills incurred if you get sick on the road. Such expenses are not generally covered by Medicare or private policies. U.K. residents can buy a travel-insurance policy valid for most vacations taken during the year in which it's purchased (but check pre-existing-condition coverage). British and Australian citizens need extra medical coverage when traveling overseas.

Always **buy travel policies directly from the insurance company**; if you buy them from a cruise line, airline, or tour operator that goes out of business you probably will not be covered for the agency or operator's default, a major risk. Before making any purchase, **review your existing health and home-owner's policies** to find what they cover away from home.

➤ Travel Insurers: In the U.S.: **Access America** (6600 W. Broad St., Richmond, VA 23230, tel. 804/285–3300 or 800/284–8300, fax 804/673–1586, www.previewtravel.com), **Travel Guard International** (1145 Clark St., Stevens Point, WI 54481, tel. 715/345–0505 or 800/826–1300, fax 800/955–8785, www.noelgroup.com).

➤ Insurance Information: In the U.K.: **Association of British Insurers** (51–55 Gresham St., London EC2V 7HQ, U.K., tel. 020/7600–3333, fax 020/7696–8999, www.abi.org.uk). In Canada: **Voyager Insurance** (44 Peel Center Dr., Brampton, Ontario L6T 4M8, Canada, tel. 905/791–8700, 800/668–4342 in Canada). In Australia: **Insurance Council of Australia** (Level 3, 56 Pitt St., Sydney NSW 2000, tel. 03/9614–1077, fax 03/9614–7924). In New

Zealand: **Insurance Council of New Zealand** (Box 474, Wellington, New Zealand, tel. 04/472–5230, fax 04/473–3011, www.icnz.org.nz).

Language

The Germans are great linguists, and you'll find that English is spoken in most hotels, restaurants, airports, stations, and museums.

LANGUAGES FOR TRAVELERS

A phrase book and language-tape set can help get you started. *Fodor's German for Travelers* (available at bookstores everywhere) is excellent.

Lodging

The hotels in our listings are divided by price into four categories: $$$$, $$$, $$, and $. *See* Where to Stay for specific prices. We always list the facilities that are available—but we don't specify whether they cost extra: when pricing accommodations, always ask what's included and what costs extra. **Ask about breakfast and bathing facilities** when booking. All hotels listed have a private bath or shower unless otherwise noted. Breakfast is usually, but not always, included. Inexpensive rooms in pensions may share a bathroom. Larger hotels often have no-smoking rooms or even no-smoking floors, so it's always worth asking for one when you reserve. Specify if you want a double bed (*Doppelzimmer*) or two single beds (*Zweibettzimmer*). Queen and king beds (*extra gross*) are rare. Smaller hotels do not provide much in terms of bathroom amenities. You may even have to request a washcloth. When you arrive, if you don't like the room you're offered, ask to see another.

You can save money by asking a reservations agent about reductions. If you have booked and plan to arrive late, let the hotel know. And if you have to cancel a reservation, inform the hotel as soon as possible, otherwise you may be charged the full amount for the unused room. To avoid scheduling a trip during a trade fair, when hotel rates soar and rooms fill, find out fair dates by contacting a German National Tourist Office.

APARTMENT RENTALS

If you want a home base that's roomy enough for a family and comes with cooking facilities, **consider a furnished rental.** These can save you money, especially if you're traveling with a group. Home-exchange directories sometimes list rentals as well as exchanges.

➤ INTERNATIONAL AGENTS: **Interhome** (1990 N.E. 163rd St., Suite 110, N. Miami Beach, FL 33162, tel. 305/940–2299 or 800/882–6864, fax 305/940–2911, www.interhome.com). **Villas International** (950 Northgate Dr., Suite 206, San Rafael, CA 94903, tel. 415/499–9490 or 800/221–2260, fax 415/499–9491, www.villasintl.com).

HOSTELS

No matter what your age, you can **save on lodging costs by staying at hostels.** Rates run DM 20/€10–DM 25/€13 for those under 27 and DM 25/€13–DM 38/€19 for older people (breakfast included). Accommodations can range from beds in single-sex, dorm-style rooms to rooms for couples and families. To stay in a hostel in Germany, you must be a member of a national hosteling association or Hostelling International (HI).

Membership in any HI national hostel association allows you to stay in HI-affiliated hostels at member rates (one-year membership is about $25 for adults). For DM 14.80/€8, the DJH Service GmbH provides a complete list of German hostels and has information on regional offices around the country. Hostels must be reserved well in advance for midsummer. To book a hostel, you must call the particular lodging directly.

➤ IN GERMANY: **DJH Service GmbH** (Postfach 1462, D–32704 Detmold, tel. 05231/74010, fax 05231/740–149, www.djh.de).

➤ ORGANIZATIONS: **Hostelling International—American Youth Hostels** (733 15th St. NW, Suite 840, Washington, DC 20005, tel.

202/783–6161, fax 202/783–6171, www.hiayh.org). **Hostelling International—Canada** (400–205 Catherine St., Ottawa, Ontario K2P 1C3, Canada, tel. 613/237–7884, fax 613/237–7868, www.hostellingintl.ca). **Youth Hostel Association of England and Wales** (Trevelyan House, 8 St. Stephen's Hill, St. Albans, Hertfordshire AL1 2DY, U.K., tel. 0870/8708808, fax 01727/844126, www.yha.org.uk). **Australian Youth Hostel Association** (10 Mallett St., Camperdown, NSW 2050, Australia, tel. 02/9565–1699, fax 02/9565–1325, www.yha.com.au). **Youth Hostels Association of New Zealand** (Box 436, Christchurch, New Zealand, tel. 03/379–9970, fax 03/365–4476, www.yha.org.nz).

HOTELS

Many major American hotel chains—Hilton, Sheraton, Holiday Inn, Best Western, Marriott—have hotels in Frankfurt. European chains are similarly well represented.

➤ **TOLL-FREE NUMBERS: Best Western** (tel. 800/528–1234, www.bestwestern.com). **Choice** (tel. 800/221–2222, www.hotelchoice.com). **Forte** (tel. 800/225–5843, www.forte-hotels.com). **Holiday Inn** (tel. 800/465–4329, www.basshotels.com). **Le Meridien** (tel. 800/543–4300, www.lemeridien-hotels.com). **Sheraton** (tel. 800/325–3535, www.starwood.com).

Mail

POSTAL RATES

Airmail letters to the United States, Canada, Australia, and New Zealand cost DM 3/€1.50; postcards, DM 2/€1. All letters to the United Kingdom cost DM 1.10/€.55; postcards, DM 1/€.50.

RECEIVING MAIL

You can arrange to have mail sent to you in care of any German post office; **have the envelope marked "Postlagernd."** This service is free, and the mail will be held for 14 days. Or you can have mail sent to any American Express office in Germany. There's no charge to cardholders, holders of American Express traveler's checks, or anyone who has booked a vacation with American Express.

Money Matters

Prices throughout this guide are given for adults. Substantially reduced fees are almost always available for children, students, and senior citizens. For information on taxes, *see* Taxes.

ATMS

Twenty-four-hour ATMs (Geldautomaten) can be accessed with PLUS or Cirrus credit and banking cards. Some German banks exact DM 4/€2–DM 10/€5 fees for use of their ATMs. Your PIN number should be set for four digits; if it's longer, ask your bank about changing it for your trip. Since some ATM keypads show no letters, know the numeric equivalent of your password.

CREDIT CARDS

All major U.S. credit cards are accepted in Germany. If you get a four-digit PIN number for your card before you leave home, you can use your credit card at German ATMs.

Throughout this guide, the following abbreviations are used: **AE,** American Express; **DC,** Diners Club; **MC,** MasterCard; and **V,** Visa.

➤ REPORTING LOST CARDS: **American Express:** tel. 01805/840–840. **Diners Club:** tel. 05921/861–234. **MasterCard:** tel. 0800/819–1040. **Visa:** tel. 08008/149–100.

CURRENCY

In the year 2002, Germany will make the final switch from the German mark to the common European euro. Though businesses, banks, and governments have been switching their books since the euro's introduction in 1999, it is now the consumer's turn. Both D-marks (DM) and euros (€) can theoretically be used until July 1, 2002, though the transition is likely to be practically in effect by March 2002. You probably will get your change in euros even if you pay in marks during the transition period. Private banks will probably charge non-customers for changing marks to euros. The Bundesbank (central bank) will exchange marks at no charge. There are about two marks to both the euro and the dollar. The euro is divided into 100 cents. There are bills of 5, 10, 20, 50, 100, and 500 euros and coins of 1, 2, 5, 10, 20, and 50 cents. At press time the euro stood at 1.06 to the U.S. dollar, .71 to the Canadian dollar, 1.59 to the British pound sterling, 1.26 to the Irish punt, .59 to the Australian dollar, .47 to the New Zealand dollar, and .14 to the South African rand. The mark is divided into 100 pfennige. There are bills of 5 (rare), 10, 20, 50, 100, 200, 500, and 1,000 marks and coins of 1, 2, 5, 10, and 50 pfennige and 1, 2, and 5 marks. At press time the mark stood at DM 2.18 to the U.S. dollar, DM 1.40 to the Canadian dollar, DM 3.15 to the British pound sterling, DM 2.48 to the Irish punt, DM 1.13 to the Australian dollar, DM .89 to the New Zealand dollar, and DM .27 to the South African rand.

CURRENCY EXCHANGE

If you are **exchanging currency from another European Union country** into German marks, do so free of charge at any branch of Germany's central bank, the **Deutsche Bundesbank** (it doesn't work the other way around, though: you cannot get Italian lire or French francs free of charge at the Deutsche Bundesbank).

For the most favorable rates, **change money through banks.** Although ATM transaction fees may be higher abroad than at home, ATM rates are excellent because they are based on wholesale rates offered only by major banks. You won't do as well at exchange booths in airports or rail and bus stations, in hotels, in restaurants, or in stores. To avoid lines at airport exchange booths, **get a bit of local currency before you leave home.**

➤ EXCHANGE SERVICES: **International Currency Express** (tel. 888/278–6628 for orders, www.foreignmoney.com). **Thomas Cook Currency Services** (tel. 800/287–7362 for telephone orders and retail locations, www.us.thomascook.com).

TRAVELER'S CHECKS

Lost or stolen checks can usually be replaced within 24 hours. To ensure a speedy refund, buy your own traveler's checks—don't let someone else pay for them: irregularities like this can cause delays. The person who bought the checks should make the call to request a refund.

Packing

What you pack depends more on the time of year than on any particular dress code. Winters can be bitterly cold; summers are warm but with days that suddenly turn cool and rainy.

Jeans are as popular in Germany as anywhere else and are perfectly acceptable for sightseeing and informal dining. In the evening, men will probably feel more comfortable wearing a jacket and tie in more expensive restaurants, although it is almost never required.

To discourage purse snatchers and pickpockets, **carry a handbag with long straps** that you can sling across your body bandolier style and with a zippered compartment for money and other valuables.

For stays in budget hotels, **take your own soap.** Many provide no soap at all or only a small bar.

In your carry-on luggage, **pack an extra pair of eyeglasses or contact lenses and enough of any medication** you take to last the entire trip. You may also ask your doctor to write a spare prescription using the drug's generic name, since brand names may vary from country to country. In luggage to be checked, **never pack prescription drugs or valuables.** To avoid customs delays, carry medications in their original packaging. And don't forget to carry with you the addresses of offices that handle refunds of lost traveler's checks. Check Fodor's How to Pack (available in bookstores everywhere) for more tips.

CHECKING LUGGAGE

How many carry-on bags you can bring with you is up to the airline. Most allow two, but not always, so make sure that everything you carry aboard will fit under your seat or in the overhead bin, and get to the gate early. Note that if you have a seat at the back of the plane, you'll probably board first, while the overhead bins are still empty.

If you are flying internationally, note that baggage allowances may be determined not by piece but by weight—generally 88 pounds (40 kilograms) in first class, 66 pounds (30 kilograms) in business class, and 44 pounds (20 kilograms) in economy.

Airline liability for baggage is limited to $1,250 per person on flights within the United States. On international flights it amounts to $9.07 per pound or $20 per kilogram for checked baggage (roughly $640 per 70-pound bag) and $400 per passenger for unchecked baggage. You can buy additional coverage at check-in for about $10 per $1,000 of coverage, but it excludes a rather extensive list of items, shown on your airline ticket.

Before departure, **itemize your bags' contents** and their worth, and label the bags with your name, address, and phone number. (If you use your home address, cover it so potential thieves can't see it readily.) Inside each bag, **pack a copy of your itinerary.** At check-in, **make sure that each bag is correctly tagged** with the destination airport's three-letter code. If your bags arrive damaged or fail to arrive at all, file a written report with the airline before leaving the airport.

Passports & Visas

When traveling internationally, **carry your passport** even if you don't need one (it's always the best form of I.D.) and **make two photocopies of the data page** (one for someone at home and another for you, carried separately from your passport). If you lose your passport, promptly call the nearest embassy or consulate and the local police.

ENTERING GERMANY

U.S., Canadian, Australian, New Zealand, and British citizens need only a valid passport to enter Germany for stays of up to 90 days.

PASSPORT OFFICES

The best time to apply for a passport or to renew is in fall and winter. Before any trip, check your passport's expiration date, and, if necessary, renew it as soon as possible.

➤ AUSTRALIAN CITIZENS: **Australian Passport Office** (tel. 131–232, www.dfat.gov.au/passports).

➤ CANADIAN CITIZENS: **Passport Office** (tel. 819/994–3500; 800/567–6868 in Canada, www.dfait-maeci.gc.ca/passport).

➤ NEW ZEALAND CITIZENS: **New Zealand Passport Office** (tel. 04/494–0700, www.passports.govt.nz).

➤ U.K. CITIZENS: **London Passport Office** (tel. 0870/521–0410, www.ukpa.gov.uk) for fees and documentation requirements and to request an emergency passport.

➤ U.S. CITIZENS: **National Passport Information Center** (tel. 900/225–5674; calls are 35¢ per minute for automated service, $1.05 per minute for operator service; www.travel.state.gov/npicinfo.html).

Rest Rooms

If there is an attendant in the rest room, he or she will likely have a plate out "primed" with one mark, which is what you should leave as well.

Safety

Frankfurt has a large drug-using community and prostitution is practiced openly, particularly in the area around the main train station. However, the district is well policed and the crime rate is no higher there than in other neighborhoods.

Senior-Citizen Travel

Frankfurt has very elaborate arrangements for seeing to the needs of resident seniors, but few of them are of much use to the visiting senior. There are no special discounts on local transportation and very few senior discounts at museums, hotels, or regular restaurants. There are, however, a number of *Seniorenrestaurants* (Senior Restaurants) where anyone over 55, including visitors, can get a good meal for DM 8/€4 to DM 10/€5. A list of such restaurants can be obtained from Frankfurter Verband für Alten- und Behindertenhilfe. This organization is also ready and willing to help seniors with any other problems they may have.

➤ **LOCAL INFORMATION: Frankfurter Verband für Alten- und Behindertenhilfe** (Mainkai 43, tel. 069/299–8070).

➤ **EDUCATIONAL PROGRAMS: Elderhostel** (11 Ave. de Lafayette, Boston, MA 02111-1746, tel. 877/426–8056, fax 877/426–2166, www.elderhostel.org).

Sightseeing Tours

BOAT TOURS

Day trips on the Main River run from March through October and leave from the Frankfurt Mainkai am Eiserner Steg, just south of the Römer complex. The Frankfurt Personenschiffahrt GmbH company has boat trips along the Main and excursions to the Rhine.

➤ **FEES & SCHEDULES: Frankfurt Personenschiffahrt GmbH** (Mainkai 36, tel. 069/281–884).

BUS TOURS

Two-and-a-half-hour city bus tours with English-speaking guides are offered throughout the year. From April through October tours leave from outside the main tourist information office at Römerberg 27 daily at 10 AM and 2 PM; all these tours leave from the south side of the train station 15 minutes later. The tour includes the price of admission to the Goethehaus and the top of the Maintower. November through March, tours leave daily at 2, stopping at 2:15 at the south side of the train station. The cost is DM 44/€22.50. Gray Line offers two-hour city tours by bus four times a day for DM 55/€28.20. They leave from the line's office at Wiesenhüttenplatz 39, or they will pick you up at an inner-city hotel.

The City Transit Authority runs a brightly painted old-time streetcar—the *Ebbelwoi Express* (Cider Express)—on weekend and holiday afternoons. Departures are from the Bornheim-Mitte U- and S-Bahn station, and the fare, DM 6/€3, includes a glass of Apfelwein.

➤ FEES & SCHEDULES: **Tourist Office** (Römerberg 27, tel. 069/2123–8708). **Verkehrsgesellschaft Frankfurt am Main** (City Transit Authority, tel. 069/2132–2425). **Gray Line** (Wiesenhüttenpl. 39, tel. 069/230–492).

EXCURSION TOURS
The Historische Eisenbahn Frankfurt runs a vintage steam train along the banks of the Main River on weekends. The train runs from the Eiserner Steg bridge west to Frankfurt-Griesham and east to Frankfurt-Mainkur. The fare is DM 6/€3.

Two companies offer tours around Frankfurt as well as farther afield. Deutsche Touring will take you to Rothenburg, Heidelberg, and the Black Forest. Gray Line has trips to the Rhine and to amusement parks as well as night club tours.

➤ FEES & SCHEDULES: **Deutsche Touring** (Am Römerhof 17, tel. 069/790–350). **Gray Line** (Wiesenhüttenpl. 39, tel. 069/230–492). **Historische Eisenbahn Frankfurt** (Eiserner Steg, tel. 069/436–093).

WALKING TOURS
The tourist office's walking tours cover a variety of topics, including Goethe, Jewish history, literature, transportation, architecture, and business. Tours can also be tailored to your interests. For an English-speaking guide, the cost is DM 200/103 plus tax for up to two hours, and DM 100/€51 per hour after that.

▶ FEES & SCHEDULES: **Tourist office** (Römerberg 27, tel. 069/2123–8849.

Students in Frankfurt

Most museums and modes of transportation have reduced prices for students, so have your student ID card handy. *See* Lodging for hostelling information.

▶ I.D.s & SERVICES: **Council Travel** (CIEE; 205 E. 42nd St., 15th floor, New York, NY 10017, tel. 212/822–2700 or 888/268–6245, fax 212/822–2699, www.councilexchanges.org) for mail orders only, in the U.S. **Travel Cuts** (187 College St., Toronto, Ontario M5T 1P7, Canada, tel. 416/979–2406 or 800/667–2887 in Canada, fax 416/979–8167, www.travelcuts.com).

Subway Travel

☞ *See* Transportation Around Frankfurt.

Taxes

All airport taxes are included in the price of your ticket. There is no special hotel tax in Germany, VAT is included in the room rate.

VALUE-ADDED TAX

Most prices you see displayed already have Germany's 16% value-added tax (VAT) included. When traveling to a non-EU country, you are entitled to a refund of the VAT you pay (multiply the price of an item by 13.8% to find out how much VAT cost is embedded in the price). Some goods, like books and antiquities, carry a 6.5% VAT as a percentage of the purchase price.

Global Refund is a VAT refund service that makes getting your money back hassle-free. The service is available Europe-wide at 130,000 affiliated stores. In participating stores, **ask for the Global Refund form** (called a Shopping Cheque). If a store is not a participating member of Global Refund, they'll probably have a form called an *Ausfuhr-Abnehmerbescheinigung*, which Global Refund can also process, for a higher fee.

When you leave the European Union, you must **show your purchases to customs officials** before they will stamp your refund form. If you are departing from Terminal 1 at Frankfurt Airport, bring your purchases to one of two areas, depending on how you've packed the goods. For items in baggage you will check, bring the baggage to the customs office in the baggage claim areas of Arrivals Halls A, B, and C (access through the Terminal Supervisor Desk); or bring your baggage to Level 3 near the Sky Line Station, B. For goods you are carrying on the plane with you, go to the customs office at Gates A 15/17, Transit Area B, near the passport control; or baggage claim area, Hall C.

If you are departing from Terminal 2, bring goods in checked baggage to the customs office in Hall D, Level 2 (opposite the Delta Airlines check-in counters). For goods you are carrying on the plane with you, go to the customs office in Hall E, Level 3 (near security control). Once the form is stamped, take it to one of the more than 700 Global Refund counters—located at every major airport and border crossing—and your money will be refunded on the spot in the form of cash, check, or a refund to your credit-card account (minus a small percentage for processing). Alternatively, you can mail your validated form to Global Refund.

➤ V.A.T. Refunds: **Global Refund** (99 Main St., Ste. 307, Nyack, NY 10960, tel. 800/566–9828, fax 845/348–1549, www. globalrefund.com).

Taxis

Cabs are not always easy to hail from the sidewalk; some stop, while others will pick up only from the city's numerous taxi stands or outside hotels or the train station. You can always order a cab. Fares start at DM 3.80/€1.95 (DM 5/€2.50 in the wee hours) and increase by a per kilometer (½ mi) charge of DM 2.80/€1.40 for the first three, DM 2.50/€1.30 thereafter. Count on paying DM 13/€6.70 for a short city ride.

➤ Taxi Companies: tel. 069/250–001 or 069/230–033.

Telephones

AREA & COUNTRY CODES

The country code for Germany is 49. When dialing a German number from abroad, drop the initial 0 from the local area code. The country code for the United States is 1.

DIRECTORY & OPERATOR ASSISTANCE

The German telephone system is fully automatic, and it's unlikely you'll have to employ the services of an operator unless you're seeking information. If you have difficulty reaching your number, call 0180/200–1033. You can book collect calls through this number to the United States but not to other countries. For information in English, dial 11837 for numbers within Germany, and 11834 for numbers elsewhere.

INTERNATIONAL CALLS

International calls can be made from just about any telephone booth in Germany. It costs only 48 pfennige/.25 per minute to call the United States, day or night, no matter how long the call lasts. Use a phone card. You can also make international calls from post offices, but you must then pay the clerk a DM 2/€1 connection fee in addition to the cost of the call. At a hotel, rates will be at least double the regular charge, so **never make international calls from your room.**

LOCAL CALLS

A local call from a telephone booth costs 20 pfennige/.10 per minute.

LONG-DISTANCE SERVICES

AT&T, MCI, and Sprint access codes make calling long-distance relatively convenient, but you may find the local access number blocked in many hotel rooms. First ask the hotel operator to connect you. If the hotel operator balks, ask for an international operator, or dial the international operator yourself. One way to improve your odds of getting connected to your long-distance carrier is to travel with more than one company's calling card (a hotel may block Sprint, for example, but not MCI). If all else fails, call from a pay phone.

➤ **ACCESS CODES:** In Germany: **AT&T Direct** (tel. 0800/888–0012). **MCI WorldCom** (tel. 0130–0012). **Sprint International Access** (tel. 0800/8880013).

MOBILE PHONES

Germany has a GSM cellphone network, which is compatible with digital mobile phones from Australia, New Zealand, the United Kingdom, and the United States. Your home network will be able to advise you what you need to do if you want to use your cellphone or pager while in Germany.

PUBLIC PHONES

Most telephone booths in Germany now are card-operated, and it's risky to assume you'll find a coin-operated booth when you need one, so **buy a phone card.** You can purchase one, among other places, at post offices, newsstands, and exchange booths. They come in denominations of DM 12/€6 and DM 50/€25, the latter good for DM 60/€30 worth of calls. Most phone booths have instructions in English as well as German. Another advantage of the card: it charges only what the call cost. Coin-operated phones, which take 10-pfennig, DM 1, and DM 5 coins, don't make change.

Time

Germany is on Central European Time, which is one hour ahead of Greenwich Mean Time, six hours ahead of Eastern Standard Time and nine hours ahead of Pacific Standard Time. Germans use military time (1 PM is indicated as 13) and write the date before the month, so October 3 will appear as 03.10.

Tipping

The service charges on bills is sufficient for most tips in your hotel, though you should **tip bellhops and porters**; DM 2/€1 per bag or service is ample. It's also customary to leave a small tip (a couple of marks per night) for the room-cleaning staff. Whether you tip the desk clerk depends on whether he or she has given you any special service. Do tip a concierge if he or she has assisted you in any way.

Service charges are included in all restaurant checks (listed as *Bedienung*), as is tax (listed as *MWST*). Nonetheless, it is customary to **round up the bill to the nearest mark or to leave about 5%** (give it to the waiter or waitress as you pay the bill; don't leave it on the table, as that's considered rude). Bartenders and servers also expect a 2%–5% tip.

In taxis **round up the fare a couple of marks** as a tip. Only give more if you have particularly cumbersome or heavy luggage.

Tours & Packages

Because everything is prearranged on a prepackaged tour or independent vacation, you'll spend less time planning—and often get it all at a good price.

For hundreds of out-of-the-ordinary tour options click on "Adventure Travel" at www.fodors.com.

BOOKING WITH AN AGENT

Travel agents are excellent resources. But it's a good idea to collect brochures from several agencies as some agents' suggestions may be influenced by relationships with tour and package firms that reward them for volume sales. If you have a special interest, **find an agent with expertise in that area**; ASTA (☞ Travel Agencies) has a database of specialists worldwide.

Make sure your travel agent knows the accommodations and other services of the place they're recommending. Ask about the hotel's location, room size, beds, and whether it has a pool, room service, or programs for children, if you care about these. Has your agent been there in person or sent others whom you can contact?

Do some homework on your own, too: local tourism boards can provide information about lesser-known and small-niche operators, some of which may sell only direct.

BUYER BEWARE

Each year consumers are stranded or lose their money when tour operators—even large ones with excellent reputations—go out of business. So **check out the operator.** Ask several travel agents about its reputation, and try to **book with a company that has a consumer-protection program.** (Look for information in the company's brochure.) In the United States, members of the National Tour Association and the United States Tour Operators Association are required to set aside funds to cover your payments and travel arrangements in the event that the company defaults. It's also a good idea to choose a company that participates in the American Society of Travel Agents' Tour Operator Program (TOP); ASTA will act as mediator in any disputes between you and your tour operator.

Remember that the more your package or tour includes the better you can predict the ultimate cost of your vacation. Make sure you know exactly what is covered, and **beware of hidden costs.** Are taxes, tips, and transfers included? Entertainment and excursions? These can add up.

➤ TOUR-OPERATOR RECOMMENDATIONS: **American Society of Travel Agents** (☞ Travel Agencies). **National Tour Association** (NTA; 546 E. Main St., Lexington, KY 40508, tel. 859/226–4444 or 800/ 682–8886, www.ntaonline.com). **United States Tour Operators Association** (USTOA; 342 Madison Ave., Suite 1522, New York, NY 10173, tel. 212/599–6599 or 800/468–7862, fax 212/599–6744, www.ustoa.com).

Train Travel to and from Frankfurt

EuroCity, InterCity, and InterCity Express trains connect Frankfurt with all German cities and many major European ones. The InterCity Express line links Frankfurt with Berlin,

Hamburg, Munich, and a number of other major hubs. All long-distance trains arrive at and depart from the Hauptbahnhof, and many also stop at the new long-distance train station at the airport. Be aware that the red-light district is just northeast of the train station. Deutsche Bahn maintains an office at the Hauptbahnhof.

BAGGAGE SERVICE

Most major train stations have luggage lockers (in four sizes). By inserting coins into a storage unit, you release the unit's key. Prices range from DM 2/€1 for a small locker to DM 8/€4 for a "jumbo" one.

The Deutsche Bahn *KurierGepäck* service will deliver your baggage from a private residence or hotel to Frankfurt Airport; delivery is guaranteed on the second weekday following pickup. Buy a *KurierGepäck* ticket at any DB ticket counter or call to schedule a pickup. The service costs DM 40/€20 for the first suitcase (with a valid ticket) and DM 30/€15 for each additional piece.

➤ BAGGAGE DELIVERY: **Deutsche Bahn** (German Rail; tel. 01805/ 4884).

FARES & SCHEDULES

A DM 7/€3.50 surcharge is added to the ticket price on all InterCity and EuroCity journeys irrespective of distance (DM 14/€7 round-trip). The charge is DM 9/€4.50 if paid on board the train. InterCity Express fares are somewhat higher than normal ones.

➤ INFORMATION AND PASSES: **DER Travel Services** (9501 W. Devon Ave., Rosemont, IL 60018, tel. 800/782–2424, fax 800/860–9944 to request a brochure, 888/337–8687 fax on demand service, www.dertravel.com). **Deutsche Bahn** (German Rail, Stephanstr. 1, D–60313 Frankfurt am Main, tel. 01805/996–633 for 24-hr hot line www.bahn.de). **Eurostar** (tel. 0870/518–6186 in the U.K.). **German Rail Passenger Services** (tel. 08702/435–363 in the U.K.).

RESERVATIONS

You need to **book seats ahead even if you are using a rail pass**; seat reservations are required on some European trains, particularly high-speed trains, and are a good idea during summer and on popular routes. You'll also need a reservation if you purchase sleeping accommodations.

If you board the train without a reserved seat, you take the chance of not getting a seat. To avoid standing in reservations lines, **make an advance reservation by phone.** Call the 24-hour hot line or reserve online at www.bahn.de/home.htm. You will then be able to collect your seat ticket from a special counter without having to wait in line. Seat reservations on all trains cost DM 5/€2.50.

➤ **RESERVATION HOT LINE:** tel. 01805/996–633.

Transportation around Frankfurt

Frankfurt's smooth-running, well-integrated public transportation system (called **RMV**) consists of the U-Bahn (subway), S-Bahn (suburban railway), Strassenbahn (streetcars), and buses. Fares for the entire system, which includes a very extensive surrounding area, are uniform, though they are based on a complex zone system. Within the time that your ticket is valid (one hour for most inner-city destinations), you can transfer from one part of the system to another.

A basic one-way ticket for a ride in the inner zone costs DM 3.70/€1.90 during the peak hours of 6 to 9 and 4 to 6:30 weekdays. (DM 3.10/€1.60 the rest of the time.) There is also a reduced *Kurzstrecke* ("short stretch") fare of DM 2.90/€1.50 (DM 2.10/€1.10 off-peak). A day ticket for unlimited travel in the inner zones costs DM 13/€6.70 and includes transport to the airport.

The Frankfurt tourist office offers a one- or two-day ticket—the **Frankfurt Card**—allowing unlimited travel in the inner zone (and to the airport) and a 50% reduction on admission to 15 museums (DM 12/€6.15 for one day, DM 19/€9.75 for two days).

If you are attending a conference in Frankfurt, go to the tourist office and ask for a Congress Ticket (DM 5/€2.60), a one-day ticket valid for unlimited travel in the city and to the airport.

PAYING

Tickets may be purchased from automatic vending machines, which are at all U-Bahn and S-Bahn stations. Each station has a list of short-stretch destinations that can be reached from it, and if you're going to one of them, press the *Kurzstrecke* button on the vending machine. There is a second vertical row of buttons for the lower children's fares. Vending machines also have an extensive list of what might be called "long-stretch" destinations; those beyond the city limits. Each has a number beside it. Press the appropriate buttons for this destination, and then for either the adult or child fare, and the proper fare will appear. If your destination isn't on either list, it's a standard fare. Machines accept coins and notes and make change. If you are caught on the subway without a ticket, there's a fine of DM 60/€30.75.

Bus drivers also sell tickets, but only if you boarded at a stop that does not have a vending machine. Weekly and monthly tickets are sold at central ticket offices and newsstands.

Travel Agencies

A good travel agent puts your needs first. Look for an agency that has been in business at least five years, emphasizes customer service, and has someone on staff who specializes in your destination. In addition, **make sure the agency belongs to a professional trade organization.** The American Society of Travel Agents (ASTA), with 27,000 agents in some 170 countries, is the largest and most influential in the field. Operating under the motto "Integrity in Travel," it maintains and enforces a strict code of ethics and will step in to help mediate any agent-client disputes if necessary. ASTA also maintains a Web site that includes a directory of agents. (If a travel agency is also acting as your tour operator, *see* Buyer Beware in Tours & Packages.)

➤ **LOCAL AGENT REFERRALS: American Society of Travel Agents** (ASTA; tel. 800/965–2782 24-hr hot line, fax 703/739–7642, www.astanet.com). **Association of British Travel Agents** (68–71 Newman St., London W1T 3AH, U.K., tel. 020/7637–2444, fax 020/7637–0713, www.abtanet.com). **Association of Canadian Travel Agents** (130 Albert St., Ste. 1705, Ottawa, Ontario K1P 5G4, Canada, tel. 613/237–3657, fax 613/237–7502, www.acta.net). **Australian Federation of Travel Agents** (Level 3, 309 Pitt St., Sydney NSW 2000, Australia, tel. 02/9264–3299, fax 02/9264–1085, www.afta.com.au). **Travel Agents' Association of New Zealand** (Box 1888, Wellington 10033, New Zealand, tel. 04/499–0104, fax 04/499–0827, www.taanz.org.nz).

➤ **LOCAL AGENTS: American Express International** (Theodor Heuss Allee 112, tel. 069/97970). **Thomas Cook** (Kaiserstr. 11, tel. 069/134–733). **Hapag-Lloyd Reisebüro** (Kaiserstr. 14, tel. 069/216–216).

Visitor Information

For advance information, write to the Tourismus und Congress GmbH Frankfurt/Main. The main tourist office is at Römerberg 27 in the heart of the Old Town. It's open weekdays 9:30–5:30, weekends 10–4. There are two other information offices. One is in the main hall of the railroad station. The other, at Zeil 94a, is open weekdays 10–6, Saturday 10–4. All three offices can help you find accommodations.

Two airport information offices can also help with accommodations. The FAG Flughafen-Information, on the first floor of Arrivals Hall B, is open daily 6:45 AM–10:15 PM. The DER Deutsches Reisebüro, in Terminal 1 Arrivals Hall B, is open weekdays 6 AM–8 PM, weekends 7 AM–1 PM.

Information about trade fairs is available from the German-American Chamber of Commerce, the Tourismus und Congress GmbH Frankfurt/Main, and the German National Tourist Office.

➤ **TOURIST INFORMATION: Tourismus und Congress GmbH Frankfurt/Main** (Kaiserstr. 56, D–60329 Frankfurt am Main, tel.

069/2123–8800, www.frankfurt.de). **Main tourist office** (Römerberg 27, tel. 069/2123–8708).

➤ **GERMAN NATIONAL TOURIST OFFICES: Australia** (Box A980, Sydney, NSW 1235, tel. 9267–8148, fax 9267–9035). **Canada** (175 Bloor St. E, Suite 604, Toronto, Ontario M4W 3R8, tel. 416/968–1570, fax 416/968–1986). **U.K.** (18 Conduit St., London W1R ODT, tel. 020/7317–0908, fax 020/7495–6129). **U.S.** (122 E. 42nd St., New York, NY 10168, tel. 212/661–7200, fax 212/661–7174, www.visits-to-germany.com).

➤ **TRADE FAIR INFORMATION: German-American Chamber of Commerce** (tel. 212/974–8830 in the U.S.; 0171/734–0543 in the U.K., www.messe–frankfurt.de).

Web Sites

Do check out the World Wide Web when planning your trip. You'll find everything from weather forecasts to virtual tours of famous cities. Be sure to **visit Fodors.com** (www.fodors.com), a complete travel-planning site. You can research prices, check out bargains, read late-breaking travel news, and book plane tickets, hotel rooms, rental cars, vacation packages, and more. In addition, you can post your pressing questions in the Travel Talk section and, in the site's Rants & Raves section, read comments about some of the restaurants and hotels in this book—and chime in yourself. Other planning tools include a currency converter and weather reports, and there are loads of links to other travel resources.

Many German tourism–related Web sites have an English-language version. The option for English is usually indicated by an icon of the American or British flag. For general information on Frankfurt, try www.visits-to-germany.com or www.frankfurt.de.

When to Go

The tourist season in Germany runs from May to late October, when the weather is at its best. It's wise to **avoid Frankfurt at**

times of major trade fairs, when attendees commandeer all hotel rooms and prices soar.

CLIMATE

Germany's climate is temperate, although cold spells can plunge the thermometer well below freezing. Summers are usually sunny and warm, though you should **be prepared for a few cloudy and wet days.** Germans measure temperature in Celsius, not Fahrenheit.

➤ FORECASTS: **Weather Channel Connection** (tel. 900/932–8437), 95¢ per minute from a Touch-Tone phone.

FRANKFURT

The following are average daily maximum and minimum temperatures for Frankfurt.

Jan.	39F	4C	May	69F	20C	Sept.	69F	21C
	30	−1		49	9		52	11
Feb.	43F	6C	June	74F	23C	Oct.	57F	14C
	31	1		55	13		44	7
Mar.	51F	11C	July	75F	24C	Nov.	45F	7C
	37	3		58	15		37	3
Apr.	59F	15C	Aug.	76F	24C	Dec.	40F	4C
	41	5		57	14		32	0

GERMAN VOCABULARY

English	German	Pronunciation
Yes/no	Ja/nein	yah/nine
Please	Bitte	bit-uh
Thank you (very much)	Danke (vielen Dank)	*dahn*-kuh (*fee*-lun-dahnk)
Excuse me	Entschuldigen Sie	ent-*shool*-de-gen zee
I'm sorry.	Es tut mir leid.	es toot meer lite
Good day	Guten Tag	*goo*-ten tahk
Good bye	Auf Wiedersehen	auf *vee*-der-zane
Mr./Mrs.	Herr/Frau	hair/frau
Miss	Fräulein	*froy*-line
Pleased to meet you.	Sehr erfreut.	zair air-*froit*
How are you?	Wie geht es Ihnen?	vee gate es *ee*-nen?
Very well, thanks.	Sehr gut, danke.	zair goot *dahn*-kuh
And you?	Und Ihnen?	oont *ee*-nen

Numbers

1	ein(s)	eint(s)
2	zwei	tsvai
3	drei	dry
4	vier	fear
5	fünf	fumph
6	sechs	zex
7	sieben	zee-ben
8	acht	ahkt
9	neun	noyn
10	zehn	tsane

Days of the Week

Sunday	Sonntag	*zone-tahk*
Monday	Montag	*moan-tahk*
Tuesday	Dienstag	*deens-tahk*
Wednesday	Mittwoch	*mit-voah*
Thursday	Donnerstag	*doe-ners-tahk*
Friday	Freitag	*fry-tahk*
Saturday	Samstag/	*zahm-stakh/*
	Sonnabend	*zonn-a-bent*

Useful Phrases

Do you speak English?	Sprechen Sie Englisch?	*shprek-hun zee eng-glish?*
I don't speak German.	Ich spreche kein Deutsch.	*ich shprek-uh kine doych*
Please speak slowly.	Bitte sprechen Sie langsam.	*bit-uh shprek-en- zee lahng-zahm*
I am American/ British	Ich bin Amerikaner(in)/ Engländer(in)	*ich bin a-mer-i-kahn-er(in)/ eng-glan-der(in)*
My name is . . .	Ich heiße . . .	*ich hi-suh*
Yes please/No, thank you	Ja bitte/Nein danke	*yah bi-tuh/nine dahng-kuh*
Where are the restrooms?	Wo ist die Toilette?	*vo ist dee twah-let-uh*
Left/right	links/rechts	*links/rechts*
Open/closed	offen/geschlossen	*O-fen/geh-shloss-en*
Where is . . .	Wo ist . . .	*vo ist*
the train station?	der Bahnhof?	*dare bahn-hof*
the bus stop?	die Bushaltestelle?	*dee booss-hahlt-uh-shtel-uh*
the subway station?	die U-Bahn- Station?	*dee oo-bahn-staht- sion*
the airport?	der Flugplatz?	*dare floog-plats*
the post office?	die Post?	*dee post*
the bank?	die Bank?	*dee banhk*
the police station?	die Polizeistation?	*dee po-lee-tsai-staht-sion*
the American/ British consulate?	das amerikanische/ britische Konsulat?	*dahs a-mare-i-kahn-ishuh/ brit-ish-uh cone-tso-laht*
the Hospital?	das Krankenhaus?	*dahs krahnk-en-house*
the telephone	das Telefon	*dahs te-le-fone*

I'd like . . .	Ich hätte gerne . . .	ich het-uh gairn . . .
a room	ein Zimmer	ein tsim-er
the key	den Schlüssel	den shluh-sul
a map	eine Stadtplan	I-nuh staht-plahn
a ticket	eine Karte	I-nuh cart-uh
How much is it?	Wieviel kostet das?	vee-feel cost-et dahs?
I am ill/sick	Ich bin krank	ich bin krahnk
I need . . .	Ich brauche . . .	ich brow-khuh
a doctor	einen Arzt	I-nen artst
the police	die Polizei	dee po-li-tsai
help	Hilfe	hilf-uh
Stop!	Halt!	hahlt!
Fire!	Feuer!	foy-er
Look out/Caution!	Achtung!/Vorsicht!	ahk-tung/for-zicht

Dining Out

A bottle of . . .	eine Flasche . . .	I-nuh flash-uh
A cup of . . .	eine Tasse . . .	I-nuh tahs-uh
A glass of . . .	ein Glas . . .	ein glahss
Ashtray	der Aschenbecher	dare Ahsh-en-bekh-er
Bill/check	die Rechnung	dee rekh-nung
Do you have . . . ?	Haben Sie . . . ?	hah-ben zee
Food	Essen	es-en
I am a diabetic.	Ich bin Diabetiker(in)	ich bin dee-ah-bet-ik-er
I am on a diet.	Ich halte Diät.	ich hahl-tuh dee-et
I am a vegetarian.	Ich bin Vegetarier(in)	ich bin ve-guh-tah-re-er
I cannot eat . . .	Ich kann . . . nicht essen	ich kan . . . nicht es-en
I'd like to order . . .	Ich möchte . . . bestellen	ich mohr-shtuh . . . buh-shtel-en
Menu	die Speisekarte	dee shpie-zeh-car-tuh
Napkin	die Serviette	dee zair-vee-eh-tuh
Separate/all	Getrennt/alles	ge-trent/ah-les
together	zusammen	tsu-zah-men

Menu Guide

English	German
Made to order	Auf Bestellung
Side dishes	Beilagen
Extra charge	Extraaufschlag
When available	Falls verfügbar
Entrées	Hauptspeisen
Home made	Hausgemacht
(Not) included	. . .(nicht) inbegriffen
Depending on the season	je nach Saison
Local specialties	Lokalspezialitäten
Set menu	Menü
Lunch menu	Mittagskarte
Desserts	Nachspeisen
Style	. . . nach . . . Art
At your choice	. . . nach Wahl
At your request	. . . nach Wunsch
Prices are . . .	Preise sind . . .
Service included	*inklusive Bedienung*
Value added tax included	*inklusive Mehrwertsteuer (Mwst.)*
Specialty of the house	Spezialität des Hauses
Soup of the day	Tagessuppe
Appetizers	Vorspeisen
Is served from . . . to . . .	Wird von . . . bis . . . serviert

Methods of Preparation

Blue (boiled in salt and vinegar)	Blau
Baked	Gebacken
Fried	Gebraten
Steamed	Gedämpft
Grilled (broiled)	Gegrillt
Boiled	Gekocht
Sauteed	In Butter geschwenkt
Breaded	Paniert
Raw	Roh

When ordering steak, the English words "rare, medium, (well) done" are used and understood in German.

Beer and Wine

English	German
A dark beer	Ein Dunkles
A light beer	Ein Helles
A mug (one quart)	Eine Maß
Draught	Vom Faß
Dark, bitter, high hops content	Altbier
Strong, high alcohol content	Bockbier (Doppelbock, Märzen)
Wheat beer with yeast	Hefeweizen
Light beer, strong hops aroma	Pils(ener)
Wheat beer	Weizen(bier)
Light beer and lemonade	Radlermaß
Rosé wine	Rosëwein
Red wine	Rotwein
White wine and mineral water	Schorle
Sparkling wine	Sekt
White wine	Weißwein
dry	herb
light	leicht
sweet	süß
dry	trocken
full-bodied	vollmundig

Fish and Seafood

Eel	Aal
Oysters	Austern
Trout	Forelle
Flounder	Flunder
Prawns	Garnelen
Halibut	Heilbutt
Herring	Hering
Lobster	Hummer
Scallops	Jakobsmuscheln
Cod	Kabeljau
Crab	Krabbe

Crayfish	Krebs
Salmon	Lachs
Spiny lobster	Languste
Mackerel	Makrele
Mussels	Muscheln
Red sea bass	Rotbarsch
Sole	Seezunge
Squid	Tintenfisch
Tuna	Thunfisch

Meats

Mutton	Hammel
Veal	Kalb(s)
Lamb	Lamm
Beef	Rind(er)
Pork	Schwein(e)

Game and Poultry

Duck	Ente
Pheasant	Fasan
Goose	Gans
Chicken	Hähnchen (Huhn)
Hare	Hase
Deer	Hirsch
Rabbit	Kaninchen
Capon	Kapaun
Venison	Reh
Pigeon	Taube
Turkey	Truthahn
Quail	Wachtel

Vegetables

Eggplant	Aubergine
Red cabbage	Blaukraut, Rotkohl
Cauliflower	Blumenkohl
Beans	Bohnen

green	*grüne*
white	*weiße*
Button mushrooms	Champignons
Peas	Erbsen
Cucumber	Gurke
Cabbage	Kohl
Lettuce	Kopfsalat
Leek	Lauch
Asparagus, peas and carrots	Leipziger Allerlei
Corn	Mais
Carrots	Mohrrüben
Peppers	Paprika
Chanterelle mushrooms	Pfifferlinge
Mushrooms	Pilze
Brussels sprouts	Rosenkohl
Red beets	Rote Beete
Celery	Sellerie
Asparagus (tips)	Spargel(spitzen)
Tomatoes	Tomaten
Cabbage	Weißkohl
Onions	Zwiebeln
Spring Onions	Frühlingszwiebeln

Condiments

Basil	Basilikum
Vinegar	Essig
Spice	Gewürz
Garlic	Knoblauch
Herbs	Kräuter
Caraway	Kümmel
Bay leaf	Lorbeer
Horseradish	Meerettich
Nutmeg	Muskatnuß
Oil	Öl
Parsley	Petersilie

Saffron	Safran
Sage	Salbei
Chives	Schnittlauch
Mustard	Senf
Artificial sweetener	Süßstoff
Cinnamon	Zimt
Sugar	Zucker
Salt	Salz

INDEX

FODOR'S POCKET FRANKFURT

EDITOR: Christina Knight

EDITORIAL CONTRIBUTOR:
Ted Shoemaker

EDITORIAL PRODUCTION:
Ira-Neil Dittersdorf

MAPS: David Lindroth, *cartographer;*
Bob Blake and Rebecca Baer, *map editors*

DESIGN: Fabrizio La Rocca, *creative director;* Tigist Getachew, *art director;* Jolie Novak, *senior picture editor;* Melanie Marin, *photo editor*

PRODUCTION/MANUFACTURING:
Robert B. Shields

Cover Photograph: Jack Fields/
Corbis

COPYRIGHT

First Edition

ISBN 0–676–90198–0

ISSN 1534–8652

IMPORTANT TIP

Although all prices, opening times, and other details in this book are based on information supplied to us at press time, changes occur all the time in the travel world, and Fodor's cannot accept responsibility for facts that become outdated or for inadvertent errors or omissions. So **always confirm information when it matters**, especially if you're making a detour to visit a specific place.

SPECIAL SALES